Think Tanks

Kubilay Yado Arin

Think Tanks

The Brain Trusts of US Foreign Policy

 Springer VS

Kubilay Yado Arin
Gräfelfing, Germany

ISBN 978-3-658-02934-0   ISBN 978-3-658-02935-7 (eBook)
DOI 10.1007/978-3-658-02935-7

The Deutsche Nationalbibliothek lists this publication in the Deutsche Nationalbibliografie; detailed bibliographic data are available in the Internet at http://dnb.d-nb.de.

Library of Congress Control Number: 2013944291

Springer VS
© Springer Fachmedien Wiesbaden 2014

Springer VS is a brand of Springer DE.
Springer DE is part of Springer Science+Business Media.
www.springer-vs.de

Acknowledgements

I wish to express my gratitude to Professors Michael Hochgeschwender, Michael Kimmage and Ursula Prutsch for their support. My special thanks go to my parents Şadan and Gülsüm Arin, to my brother Kutay, to my sisters Kutlay and Dolunay and to my cousins Izlem and Imsel.

Dr. Kubilay Yado Arin

Contents

Think Tanks, the Brain Trusts of US Foreign Policy

At the start of the twentieth century, the workings of government became increasingly difficult to understand. The over-burdened policy-makers dealt with too much information to analyse domestic bargaining and to understand the conceptual frameworks of international negotiations.[1] Most governmental agencies and congressional staff did very little original research and they turned to governmental research organisations, think tanks and interest groups for information and analysis.[2] While an exact definition of the term think tank is problematic, their role - what think tanks do - appears more straight forward: organising seminars and conferences, publishing books, papers, reports and journals and encouraging their fellows to write op-ed articles for newspapers on public affairs.[3] Think tanks and their researchers provide much needed explanation of foreign and domestic policies. Diane Stone uses a broad policy network approach, the models of policy communities, advocacy coalitions and policy entrepreneurs to highlight think tanks activities and motives.[4]

Unlike European parties that do provide policy advice, politicians in the White House and on Capitol Hill are not forced to obey the party platform. The weak party discipline often encourages US congressmen and members of government to ask for policy expertise from think tanks. Many presidents have consulted think tanks for policy advise and for ideological coherence. Indeed, the American Presidents have employed experts from think tanks to serve in senior positions in their government. In fact, policy-makers look for advise to idea factories and their scholars resulting from the decentralisation and fragmentation of the American political system. In a system based on separate branches sharing powers, and one in which policy-makers are not limited by the programs of po-

---

[1] Wallace, William: Conclusion. Ideas and Influence. In: Stone, Diane/ Denham, Andrew/ Garnett, Mark (Eds.): Think Tanks Across Nations. Manchester, Manchester University Press 1998, pp. 223-230, (p. 229 -230).
[2] McGann, James G.: The Competition for Dollars, Scholars and Influence in the Public Policy Research Industry . Lanham, University Press of America, 1995, pp. 42-43.
[3] Ricci, David: The Transformation of American Politics. The New Washington and the Rise of Think Tanks. New Haven, Yale University Press, 1993, p. 1.
[4] Stone. Diane: Introduction. Think Tanks, Policy Advice, and Governance. In: Stone, Diane/ Denham, Andrew (eds.): Think Tank Traditions, Policy Research, and the Politics of Ideas. Manchester, Manchester University Press 2004, pp. 1-16 (pp. 1-2).

litical parties, think tanks can communicate their ideas through multiple channels to several hundred law-makers.[5] Over the years, writers have described think tanks by framing their source of funds, degree of independence, type of research, tax status, organisational structure, affiliation or political orientation.[6] Not the unwillingness of the Brookings Institution to become politically active makes it different from advocacy think tanks but the value it puts on medium- and long-term research. In few words, unlike advocacy think tanks like the Heritage Foundation, which supplies policy-makers with short-term information, many early think tanks give attention to a broad scope of issues relevant for the policy-makers on the long run.[7]

> „Think Tanks that follow the realist or neo-conservative school in defense and foreign policy are categorized as conservative, while those that generally represent a more liberal internationalist approach are categorized as progressive."[8]

The thesis thus focuses on think tanks, foundations, individual donors, and the role of experts and ideas in the American policy process.[9] The advocacy coalition approach provides a concept for the analysis of knowledge utilisation over the long term. Think tanks like CFR and Carnegie Endowment operate as policy forum in creating cross-coalition learning. Scholars, politicians and journalists from different political orientations were "socialised" into the policy discourse through their participation in think tank initiatives. Thus think tanks have at times influence in the context of competition between advocacy coalitions. As a consequence, there exists a symbiotic relationship between interests and knowledge.[10] From this perspective, the thesis analyses the influence of think tanks, elite policy planning organisations, on US foreign policy from Clinton to Bush Jr.[11]

---

[5] Abelson, Donald E./ Carberry, Christine M.: Policy Experts in Presidential Campaigns. A Model of Think Tank Recruitment. Presidential Studies Quarterly, 1997, 27 (4), pp. 679 – 697.
[6] Ibid., p. 11.
[7] Abelson, Donald E.: Do Think Tanks Matter? Assessing the Impact of Public Policy Institutes. 2nd Edition. Montreal, McGill-Quenn's University Press 2009, p. 23
[8] Ibid., p. 25.
[9] Abelson, Donald E. A Capitol Idea: Think Tanks and U.S. Foreign Policy. Montreal and Kingston: McGill-Queen's University Press, 2006.
[10] Sabatier, P.A./Jenkins-Smith, H.C. (eds.): Policy Change and Learning. An Advocacy Coalition Approach. Boulder, Westview Press, 1993
[11] Abelson, Donald E.: Think Tanks in the United States. In Diane Stone, Andrew Denham and Mark Garnett (eds): Think Tanks Across Nations: A Comparative Approach. Manchester: Manchester University Press, 1998: 107-126. Abelson, Donald E. and Evert A. Lindquist: Think Tanks Across North America. In: R. Kent Weaver and James G. McGann (eds): Think Tanks and Civil Societies: Catalyst for Ideas and Action. New Jersey: Transaction Publishers, 2000: 37-66.

As David Ricci has pointed out, while think tanks operate in Washington's political affairs, their existence there is hardly brought up in reference books on American politics. Political scientists, in his opinion, have not yet illustrated Washington think tanks and their recent proliferation as a new, important and institutional force in American policy-making.[12] Think tanks deal in soft power (a term coined by Joseph Nye) in forming policy agendas, in questioning the terminology and conventional wisdom of policy debate, and in affecting the thinking of the policy-makers. These are all noticeable roles, the functions of which are harder to find than the direct impact of hard political bargaining, but which devise the political arrangement within which political bargaining is organised in modern political systems.[13]

> „The term ‚market liberal' will be used interchangeably with libertarian to describe institutes or individuals informed by classical liberal principles and free market economics. In America, the term 'liberal' has been appropriated by US social democrats also known as 'progressives', while social democracy is sometimes equated with socialism. The label of liberalism emerged in the context of the new policies associated with the Roosevelt Administration and the New Deal. Those critics of the Great Society programmes are generally described as neoconservative, for example, those at institutes such as Heritage who are informed by libertarian and conservative thought."[14]

Presidential candidates and members of Congress founded think tanks or used them not only for their political expertise but to avoid limits of campaign finance laws on donations. For non-profit organisations there is no limitation on donations. Thus donors can support their candidate's election campaign and profit from their tax-exempt status while meeting the official at a think tank. Think tanks serve as election teams.[15] What is forgotten is legitimate and respectful policy advise.[16] As there is no civil service in the US, think tank scholars need to form an alliance with policy-makers to promote their careers in the US administration.[17]

---

[12] Ricci, David: The Transformation of American Politics. The New Washington and the Rise of Think Tanks. New Haven, Yale University Press, 1993, p. 2.

[13] Wallace, William: Conclusion. Ideas and Influence. In: Stone, Diane/ Denham, Andrew/ Garnett, Mark (Eds.): Think Tanks Across Nations. Manchester, Manchester University Press 1998, pp. 223-230, (p. 224).

[14] Stone, Diane: Capturing the Political Imagination. Think Tanks and the Policy Process. London, Frank Cass 1996, p. 25.

[15] Abelson, Donald E.: Do Think Tanks Matter? Assessing the Impact of Public Policy Institutes. 2nd Edition. Montreal, McGill-Quenn's University Press 2009, p. 90.

[16] Gehlen, Martin: Kulturen der Politkberatung – USA. In: Bröchler, Stephan/ Schützeichel, Rainer (eds.): Politikberatung. Stuttgart 2008, pp. 480 – 492 (p. 486).

[17] Thunert, Martin: Think Tanks in Deutschland – Berater der Politik? APuZ B51/2003, pp. 30 – 38 (p. 35).

The Progressive Policy Institute was founded as a branch of the Democratic Leadership Council in 1989. When Bill Clinton, former Chairman of the DLC, made up his mind to run for the presidency in 1992, the PPI spotted the right candidate to promote its progressive mission. Since Clinton endorsed the PPI's blueprint Mandate for Change, a reform of government, many journalists concluded that the PPI's views would dominate Washington's agenda. Most notably, the PPI believes in restoring the American dream by accelerating economic growth, educational excellence, expanding opportunity and enhancing financial and personal security. Moreover, crime prevention, health care and environmental safety found their way on Clinton's New Democrat platform. The PPI also asserts that global order can be supported by building new international structures based on economic and political freedom. The PPI research demands a new progressive politics for the US while modeling its marketing strategy similar to the Heritage Foundation and the Cato Institute.[18]

Whereas The Project for the New American Century shared the same address with the American Enterprise Institute and the Weekly Standard, edited by William Kristol, chairman of PNAC. Its Statement of Principles was openly endorsed not only by George W. Bush but also raised the Clinton administration's attention as early as 1997. The PNAC advanced a neo-Reaganite policy of military strength and moral clarity to maintain the global leadership of the U.S. in the new century. Dick Cheney, Donald Rumsfeld, Paul Wolfowitz, and Jeb Bush shared and signed its principles. When Bush developed his doctrine to promote and protect US security interests, the PNAC offered the justification for the administration's invasion in Afghanistan and Iraq. After the tragic events of 9/11, this small think tank with powerful ties to the Bush White House came into the national spotlight. Indeed, some journalists assumed that the PNAC had laid the foundations for the Bush Doctrine.[19]

The thesis examines whether the reference to the historical division of the domestic and foreign portfolios circumvents the system of checks and balances. Did US foreign policy become the executive's domain in the war on terror without congressional control? Did the Democrat administration under Clinton subordinate domestic politics to foreign policy in the war on terror?[20] Was there a shift of primacy from domestic politics to foreign policy under the Clinton administration that continued under the Bush administration? Referring to Montesquieu's argumentation of the executive's right to "instant action" this

---

[18] Abelson, Donald E.: Do Think Tanks Matter? Assessing the Impact of Public Policy Institutes. 2nd Edition. Montreal, McGill-Quenn's University Press 2009, p. 189.
[19] Ibid., pp. 41-43.
[20] Hendrickson, Ryan: The Clinton Wars – The Constitution, Congress, and War Powers, Nashville: Vanderbildt University Press, 2002.

shift of paradigm is made legitimate.[21] Following question remains to be answered: can an imperial overstretch in US foreign policy be effectively stopped by domestic mechanisms? Increasing concern for the compliance to international law and cooperation with multilateral institutions may demand a stronger domestic control of American foreign policy.[22] Particularly problematic seems to be the exclusion of Congress in the process of foreign policymaking which is attributed to the undue political advise from think tanks exclusively given to the executive.[23] Therefore, political scientists focus their analyses on how the decision-making between the White House, the National Security Council, the State Department and Pentagon evolves.[24]

In this context, scholars scrutinise how the rule of law, international law, human rights, the system of checks and balances and the international obligations to the United Nations were handled in the war on terror.[25] The US constitution, the submittal to international law and the construction of strong international institutions such as the United Nations implied that President Clinton and his predecessor Bush sr. felt obliged to respect their allies' opinion in order to build great coalitions.[26] Thus, the dissertation tries to prove how the change from a reactive to a more proactive national security from the liberal presidency of Clinton to the neoconservative presidency of Bush Jr. can be deduced from their different political agendas during their administrations.[27]

---

[21] Sheffer, Martin S.: Presidential War Powers and the War on Terrorism: Are We Destined to Repeat Our Mistakes? In: Davis, John (ed.): The Global War on Terrorism: Assessing the American Response. New York 2004, pp. 27-44 (p. 28).
[22] Weller, Christoph: Machiavellistische Außenpolitik - Altes Denken und seine US-amerikanische Umsetzung, In: Hasenclever, Andreas / Wolf, Klaus Dieter / Zürn, Michael (eds.): Macht und Ohnmacht internationaler Institutionen. Frankfurt a.M./New York: Campus, 2007, pp. 81-114, (p. 81).
[23] Glaab, Manuela/ Metz, Almut: Politikberatung und Öffentlichkeit. In: Falk, Svenja (eds.): Handbuch Poltikberatung. Wiesbaden 2006, pp. 161-172 (p. 166).
[24] Rubenstein, Richard E..: Die US-amerikanischen Wahlen. Aussichten für eine neue amerikanische Außenpolitik. Fokus Amerika der Friedrich-Ebert-Stiftung (Nr. 2), Washington, DC 2008. p. 5-6.
[25] Rivlin, Benjamin: UN Reform from the Standpoint of the United States: A Presentation Made At The United Nations University on 25 September 1995, Tokyo Japan, UN University Lectures 11. In: www.unu.edu/unupress/lecture11.html
[26] Jervis, Robert: American Foreign Policy in a New Era. New York 2005, p. 91.
[27] Arin, Kubilay Yado: Die Rolle der Think Tanks in der US-Außenpolitik. Von Clinton zu Bush Jr. Wiesbaden, VS Springer 2013.

Methodological Approach: Typologies of Think Tanks

Unlike Stone, Donald Abelson applies a typology of think tanks by focusing on four distinctive periods of think tanks development to recognise the major features of think tanks connected with the four time periods: 1900 – 46, 1947 - 1970, 1978 - 89 and 1990 - 2009. To clarify the typology, some of the most prominent think tanks are profiled. Donald Abelson supports Weaver's identification of three types of think tanks in the policy-making community: universities without students (e.g. CFR and Brookings), government contractors (RAND or CSIS) and advocacy tanks (AEI and Heritage Foundation).[28]

After World War I, domestic and foreign policy challenges led to the creation of the Carnegie Endowment for International Peace (1910), the Hoover Institution on War, Revolution and Peace (1919) and the Council on Foreign Relations (1921). As a result of the United States' emergence as a global power a small but influential elite set out to challenge American tendency toward isolationism. Internationally, there appeared to be a clear mandate for greater American involvement in global affairs, the foreign policy establishment wanted to convince political elites and the American public that it was in America's interest to play a greater role in international politics.[29]

Since the turn of the 19th-20th century, think tanks have partially filled the need for independent analysis and thought. The creation of independent research institutes supported by private donations to conduct policy research and provide a forum for ideas and debate is a strongly American characteristic that originates from the nation's democratic, pluralistic and philanthropic tradition. Think tanks propose through independent and neutral research policy ideas to solve public problems or needs. This reasoned value-neutral approach to research has increased their influence in the policymaking community. As non-profit organisations, they are not controlled by the government and are not, in the most

---

[28] Abelson, Donald E.: Do Think Tanks Matter? Assessing the Impact of Public Policy Institutes. 2nd Edition. Montreal, McGill-Quenn's University Press 2009, p. 18.
[29] Mcgann, James G.: The Competition for Dollars, Scholars and Influence in the Public Policy Research Industry . Lanham, University Press of America, 1995, p.46.

cases, aligned with any political party or special interest.[30] By comparing liberal think tanks created in the first decades of the twentieth century such as Brookings and CFR to those neoconservative advocacy think tanks comprising the AEI and the Heritage Foundation, one can observe the transformation of think tanks from non-partisan research institutes to openly ideological organisations committed to influencing the nation's agenda. Think tanks created during the Progressive Era placed more importance on providing government officials with policy expertise than to lobbying members of Congress and the executive or satisfying their donors. Devoid of the partisan interest of American politics they developed own areas of expertise, the first think tanks were devoted to the progress of knowledge. Nonetheless, think tanks should not be seen "as the sole guardians of the public interest without any political motivations".[31]

Think tanks, such as the Brookings Institution or AEI, represent universities without students that target with their long-term research the political climate and receive most gifts from a variety of donors in order to avoid client intrusion over certain advise.[32] While typologies of think tanks have some use and validity for explanational purposes, they should not be interpreted too literally. For instance, the Heritage Foundation, normally considered an advocacy think tank has also published some research resembling those studies of universities without students. Therefore Stone argues that models like Weaver's or McGann's do not allow hybrid forms.[33] Instead the term think tank is used to refer to institutions whose aims may change over time and whose researchers may become aligned to one another only shortly and for personal convenience.[34]

Many think tanks conduct research in a simplified form.[35] At one side, policy institutes become indistinct with interest groups that are increasingly recognising the value of research and analysis in policy debate. At another side, think tanks cooperate with universities, while at another border they seem to become extra-political campaigning groups.[36] Some think tanks such as the Heritage Foundation have predictable policy findings. According to Diane Stone,

---

[30] Ibid., pp. 39-42.

[31] Abelson, Donald E: Think Tanks in the United States. In: Stone, Diane/ Denham, Andrew/ Garnett, Mark (eds.): Think Tanks Across Nations. A Comparative Approach. Manchester, Manchester University Press 1998, pp. 107 – 126, (pp. 107- 110)

[32] Ricci, David: The Transformation of American Politics. The New Washington and the Rise of Think Tanks. New Haven, Yale University Press, 1993, p. 20.

[33] Stone, Diane: Old Guard versus New Partisans. Think Tanks in Transition. Australian Journal of Political Science 1991, 26 (2), pp. 197 -213 (p. 201).

[34] Ricci, David: The Transformation of American Politics. The New Washington and the Rise of Think Tanks. New Haven, Yale University Press, 1993, p. 21.

[35] Stone, Diane: Capturing the Political Imagination. Think Tanks and the Policy Process. London, Frank Cass 1996, p. 12.

[36] Ibid, p.1.

their predictable positions arise not from vested interest but rather from a conservative set of principles and underlying ideology.[37] Transition tanks have emerged to provide advice for new incoming presidents. Presidential hopefuls set up their own think tank to develop policy agendas but into which they can channel campaign contributions. The non-profit status of the think tank allows the candidate to avoid compliance with federal limits on campaign contributions. Contrary to Abelson, Stone does not recognise in transition or candidate tanks research institutes but election platforms of the candidates for promoting their message und win the elections.[38] The thesis will illustrate the theoretical and methodological approaches by examining how policy-planning organisations reshaped the foreign policy agendas from a time of political transformation under Clinton to international crises under Bush Jr.[39]

Think tanks serve in the advocacy coalition approach of Sabatier and Jenkins-Smith as agents of learning. By acting as policy forum they generate cross-coalition learning, have long-term impact on policy analysis and operate within and restrain their activity to advocacy coalitions for policy change and knowledge utilisation. As a consequence there exists a symbiotic relationship between interests and knowledge.[40] These organisations play important roles in serving as a forum for debate, generating debate and developing medium-to-long-term ideas rather than following short-term policy goals.[41] Throughout the book, views of think tank scholars (from AEI, CFR, Heritage Foundation, Brookings and Hoover Institutions) on foreign policy and national security are related to real-world developments (World War I and II, Cold War and the war on terror).[42]

By the late 1970s, Capitol Hill had been flooded with highly aggressive advocates of ideology, commonly known as advocacy think tanks. Dissatisfied with domestic and foreign affairs, advocacy think tanks struggled to become integrated in decision-making. Rather than pursuing scholarly research in public service, their ambition rested in political advocacy. Think tanks like the Heritage

---

[37] Ibid, p.14.
[38] Ibid, p.17.
[39] Abelson, Donald E. "In the Line of Fire: Think Tanks, the War on Terror and Anti-Americanism," in Richard Higgott and Ivana Malbasic (eds), The Political Consequences of Anti-Americanism. London: Routledge, 2008, pp. 44-57.
[40] Sabatier, P.A./Jenkins-Smith, H.C. (eds.): Policy Change and Learning. An Advocacy Coalition Approach. Boulder, Westview Press, 1993
[41] Stone. Diane: Introduction. Think Tanks, Policy Advice, and Governance. In: Stone, Diane/ Denham, Andrew (eds.): Think Tank Traditions, Policy Research, and the Politics of Ideas. Manchester, Manchester University Press 2004, pp. 1-16.
[42] Abelson, Donald E.: A War of Ideas: Think tanks and Terrorism. Policy Options, 28 (3) March 2007, pp. 75-78.

Foundation increasingly looked alike interest groups and political action committees by lobbying decision-makers to implement ideologically compatible policies with their values and those shared by their corporate donors. In short, advocacy think tanks did not devote scholarly attention to their research, but strived to convey their conservative mission to the voters.[43]

In assessing the influence of think tanks in government policy, scholars can interview or send questionnaires to both members of Congress and think tank experts involved in particular policy debate to determine how extensive a role think tanks played. Furthermore, they can compare the policy recommendations proposed by think tanks to the actual decisions made by government. Moreover, by assessing materials stored at the Library of Congress, it is possible to acquire a far more comprehensive understanding of the key actors that helped mould administration agendas. In fact, these themes are frequently evoked in newspapers before elections. Think tanks have become permanent fixtures in the policy-making process. That is why researchers must determine the most effective methods to evaluate their behavior.[44]

Think tanks originally educated, informed und partially lobbied among government representatives, members of Congress, high-ranking bureaucrats and journalists. Politicians and their advisers are nowadays deeply integrated in networks.[45] The distinction between experts and advocates is thin which endangers the academic standards of policy innovation. "If trusted research and analysis is not available the foundation of policy decision becomes money, interests and lobbyists".[46] During the twentieth century, research was increasingly considered in ideological terms and distribution to the public than by its value-neutral nature.[47] The thesis thus looks at evolving perspectives and policy debates in the substantive areas of domestic economics, political institutions and democratic practices and to the elite regroupment of neoconservatives against liberals with a concern on the polarisation of American politics and its implications for the American democracy. Even those think tanks that by their mission sought to maintain a balance or neutrality in their research were regularly perceived by policy makers and funders as ideologically aligned in some way.

---

[43] Abelson, Donald E: Think Tanks in the United States. In: Stone, Diane/ Denham, Andrew/ Garnett, Mark (eds.): Think Tanks Across Nations. A Comparative Approach. Manchester, Manchester University Press 1998, pp. 107 – 126, (p. 113).
[44] Ibid. p. 124.
[45] Abelson, Donald E. "Think Tanks and U.S. Foreign Policy: An Historical View." U.S. Foreign Policy Agenda: An Electronic Journal of the U.S. Department of State, 7 (3), November 2002: 9-12.
[46] Rich, Andrew: Think Tanks, Public Policy and the Politics of Expertise. Cambridge, Cambridge University Press 2004, pp. 214 -215.
[47] Ibid..

Policy Communities, Advocacy Coalitions and Epistemic Communities

Think tanks' influence has more to do with the way in which think tanks successfully interact in policy networks (including policy communities, advocacy coalitions and discourse coalitions). A policy network incorporates actors from both inside and outside government to facilitate decision-making and implementation. Through networks, think tanks can be integrated into the policy making process. Pluralists do usually stress the openness and informal participation in decision-making offered by networks. Yet, it has also been recognised that policy networks can inhibit demands for change to preserve benefits and privileges. Networks undermine political duty by locking out the electorate.[48]

> „As noted, scholars have treated think tanks as elite organisations with close and lasting ties to policy-makers, or like pluralists as one of many nongovernmental organisations that seek to influence public policy, or as institutes composed of experts that frequently participate in policy or epistemic communities."[49]

Although pluralists assume that public policy is an outcome of group competition, they do not analyse if some organisations may be better positioned to influence policy decisions than others because of greater membership, larger budgets and bigger staff. Think tanks use their expertise and close ties to policymakers to subdue their competitors in prestige and status in the policy-making community.[50] Institutes build an infrastructure to maintain contact and keep actors informed on their research. Networking is not put on par with political influence, but it raises the effectiveness of think tanks in implementing policies. Networks are conceived as a source of innovation where intellectual authority can be used to support policy decisions.

---

[48] Rhodes, R.A..W./Marsh, David: New Studies in the Study of Policy Networks. European Journal of Policy Research 1992, 21, pp. 181 – 205.
[49] Ricci, David M: The Transformation of American Politics. The New Washington and the Rise of Think Tanks. New Haven, Yale University Press, 1993, p. 14.
[50] Abelson, Donald E.: Do Think Tanks Matter? Assessing the Impact of Public Policy Institutes. 2nd Edition. Montreal, McGill-Quenn's University Press 2009, p. 53.

Policy entrepreneurs pursue networking in order to capture political agendas thereby knowledge becomes politicised by think tanks. Establishing links with the media, trade unions, political parties, bureaucrats and departments is essential for their networking and coalition building. The informal links to politicians enable scholars to promote ideas and mould public opinion. Think tanks bring their expert knowledge into the public sector by serving in government agencies and congressional committees.[51] Public policy research institutions are non-profit organisations that generate policy-oriented research, ideas, analysis, formulations and recommendations on domestic and international issues. In addition, these institutions act often as a bridge between the academic and policy communities, translating research into a language that is open to policymakers.[52]

Within policy communities, think tank scholars likely obtain insider status as they share common values with the political class. The advocacy coalition approach places high value on a long-term function as educator in altering policies. Furthermore this approach highlights the role of beliefs, values and ideas as a neglected dimension of policy-making. The epistemic community concept concentrates on the specific roles of knowledge or experts in the policy process. In discourse coalitions, think tanks concentrate on advocates, researchers and analysts to devise solutions to policy problems.[53]

The foreign policy think tanks function as "brokers of ideas" between the "ivory towers of academia" and "the policy-making world of government" in the "increasingly competitive market-place of ideas".[54] Think tanks operate on their own to influence decision-making. They are in competition with other think tanks to attract political and media attention as well as financial support. Consequently, think tanks pursue to gain media visibility by advocating key issues in the political debate. Think tanks thus gain an audience in government and media circles. Think tanks draw upon a network on scholars based in universities, bureaucracies and industry to devise solutions. In conferences, seminars or task forces, think tanks bring together people from government, congress, the military or bureaucracy with the aim of alignment among actors with common objectives

---

[51] Stone, Diane/ Garnett, Mark: Introduction: Think Tanks, Policy Advice and Governance. In. Stone, Diane/ Denham, Andrew/ Garnett, Mark (Eds.): Think Tanks Across Nations. Manchester, Manchester University Press 1998, pp. 1-20, (pp. 16 -17).

[52] McGann, James G.: The Competition for Dollars, Scholars and Influence in the Public Policy Research Industry . Lanham, University Press of America, 1995, pp. 31-32.

[53] Stone, Diane/ Garnett, Mark: Introduction: Think Tanks, Policy Advice and Governance. In. Stone, Diane/ Denham, Andrew/ Garnett, Mark (Eds.): Think Tanks Across Nations. Manchester, Manchester University Press 1998, pp. 1-20, (pp. 15 -16).

[54] McGann, James G.: The Competition for Dollars, Scholars and Influence in the Public Policy Research Industry . Lanham, University Press of America, 1995, p.16.

and interests.[55] The concept of the epistemic communities provides according to Diane Stone a better explanation for the role of think tanks among groups of policy experts. An epistemic community comprises an interdisciplinary network of specialists who share a common world view and aim to implement their ideas into public policy and government projects. Think tanks represent a type of community where scholars can be identified. By comparing the effectiveness and motivations of research institutes one can determine their differing impact. Therefore, these institutes may influence the political thinking and alter the public opinion when the issue is brought up by an epistemic community. Research institutes can help epistemic communities to win political support among powerholders. Think tanks concentrate their efforts to raise the public's awareness to new problems with the aim of legitimising their solutions by the state. Nevertheless, the ability of epistemic communities to shape the political agenda will never be perfect. The concept of political networks in the form of epistemic/ policy communities and discourse coalitions only serves the function to illustrate the political relevance of think tanks.[56]

In addition, their influence on public opinion can be measured through the number of publications, media presentations, conferences, seminars or in the internet.[57] As specified by Diane Stone, ideas need organisations, scholars and intellectuals who convey them to decision-makers. For this reason, think tanks increasingly play an active political role that interferes with their analyses for policy-makers in the decision-making process. Furthermore, they indirectly shape public opinion through their ideas. The research institutes inject their ideas into policymaking. For leading academics, managers and journalists think tanks offer a base for marketing their policy reforms. Diane Stone blames the short-sightedness of political scientists who often ignore the institutes' achievements as source for policy innovation, as educators of the public and as policy advisers.[58]

Sabatier's and Jenkins-Smith's theoretical approach the advocacy coalition provides a conceptual framework for analysing long-term use and application of knowledge. The idea factories act as communication panels concerning appropriate policy measures between researchers, journalists and policy-makers. In the advocacy coalition approach all political tendencies are integrated in the political discourse by initiatives of think tanks for certain actors. Their participation in seminars and conferences may lead to a socialisation of policy coalitions,

---

[55] Stone and Garnett, Introduction, pp. 16 -17.
[56] Stone, Diane: Capturing the Political Imagination, p. 3.
[57] Braml, Josef: Deutsche und amerikanische Think Tanks. Voraussetzungen für ihr Wirken. Wissenschaft und Frieden 2004 – 4: Think Tanks. pp. 1-5 (p. 1).
[58] Stone, Capturing the Political Imagination, p. 1.

that also causes a learning effect over limitations by groups and political orientation. The institutes shape the competition of advocacy coalitions resulting in a
policy change. As agents of learning, they start a learning effect with their long-
term analysis and the application of their knowledge crosses the limits of coalitions and political activities. Hence, both authors talk of a symbiotic relationship
between interests and knowledge.[59] Contravening with Sabatier's and Jenkins-
Smith's statement Kingdon, however, makes policy entrepreneurs responsible,
i.e. policy-makers, career bureaucrats, lobbyists, academics and journalists, for
political advocacy of problem solutions. Increasing lobbyism can build coalitions
between elected officials having the implication that a consensus develops at the
costs of policy alternatives. If enough resources are mobilised, negotiations and
bargaining will add up to policy implementation, otherwise proposals will disap-
pear from the agenda. Defining a problem precedes the placement on the public
agenda, whereas alternatives require a long-term advocacy before a chance of
solution unfolds. Policy entrepreneurs pursue the goal to convince policy-makers
of their definition of a policy problem. On that account, they evaluate government performance in letters, complaints and during visits to officials for steering
the agenda. By sensibilising the public, specialists attempt to convey their issues
to the political community. For this reason, scholars in think tanks bind solutions
to problems, bring problems into the awareness of political circles and prompt
decision-makers to implement their policy proposals in the pursuit of their interests.[60]

Despite this criticism, Stone claims that epistemic communities function
as medium that assess the political agenda, limit the debate to important topics
and raise the level of political awareness among power-holders. Research institutes show their full potential inside an epistemic community. Though she cri-
tisises the networking activities of certain institutes that are occupied with research brokerage to inform politics. In this context, Stone also mentions policy
entrepreneurs in the guise of philanthropic training centers that haven taken over
the political advocacy of a cause in the war of ideas. Thus, their ideas, policy
proposals and their impact on the agenda and public opinion must be examined.[61] Referring to Gehlen, policy proposals of these institutes have no distinct
function in the policy stream. They do not provide alternative expertise anymore,
they do not enhance knowledge or broaden the scope of problem solutions. Instead, they are primarily subordinate to the sole aim of promoting their own values.

---

[59] Sabatier and Jenkins-Smith, Policy Change, p.1.
[60] Kingdon, Agendas, pp. 213-215.
[61] Stone, Capturing the Political Imagination. p. 6.

Theoretical Explanations for the Political Influence of Think Tanks

The foundation of the first foreign policy think tanks (Carnegie, Hoover, and CFR) after World War I, can be shown in the academic contributions to the study of International Relations. The diplomats were educated as practitioners with analyses and theories out of research institutes, which confirms their political role in foreign relations. Think tanks are illustrated as contemporary mode of interaction between scientific research and the political domain. Think tanks filter immense data on knowledge, facts, and information, which they refine for policymaking.[62] „Foreign Policy think-tanks burgeoned as the USA became a hegemonic power in world affairs and as the Cold War developed."[63]

It is almost impossible, according to Donald Abelson, to assess exactly the impact of certain institutes on specific policy decisions. Because of the methodological difficulties, it is hard to establish a causal relationship between policy recommendations by different think tanks and decisions made by policymakers. It is however possible to draw conclusions on their role in the political process by showing the interconnectedness of think tanks with politicians and the public. Competing for power and prestige at the local, state and national level in the US, think tanks try to mould public opinion and shape public policy.[64]

> „Scholars use various indicators such as media citations, parliamentary and congressional testimony, and consultations with government departments and agencies to evaluate the impact or relevance of think tanks at particular stages of the policy-making process. The amount of media exposure think tanks generate and the number of appearances they make before legislative committees may provide some insight into how visible particular organisations are."[65]

---

[62] Stone, Diane: Capturing the Political Imagination. Think Tanks and the Policy Process. London, Frank Cass 1996, pp. 6-7.
[63] Ibid. p. 18.
[64] Abelson, Donald E: Think Tanks in the United States. In: Stone, Diane/ Denham, Andrew/ Garnett, Mark (eds.): Think Tanks Across Nations. A Comparative Approach. Manchester, Manchester University Press 1998, pp. 107 – 126, (p. 107 -108)
[65] Abelson, Donald E.: Do Think Tanks Matter? Assessing the Impact of Public Policy Institutes. 2nd Edn, Montreal, McGill-Queen's University Press 2009, p. 15.

Measuring the political impact of think tanks on US foreign policy demands the examination of the complex decision-making process between the White House and the departments. It stays, however, difficult to ascertain their influence on policy-makers through congressional testimonies and personal contacts. But the collaboration of think tank experts under the presidencies of Clinton and Bush Jr. may prove their political role. Prominent names of former government officials who work as fellows in think tanks are always cited in the annual reports of these organisations as indicators for informal political influence. The same method is applied to their former staff who now serve in high-ranking administration posts.[66]

Congress, bureaucracy, political parties, think tanks and media obviously play a major role in the foreign policy process in the United States. For analysing their influence on US foreign policy scholars use the method of policy cycle which concentrates on the institutional origin and setting of American diplomacy. The competition between Congress and the governmental departments and agencies offers thinks tanks the opportunity to shape foreign policy through their policy proposals. Their impact on decision-making results from personal contacts to the White House, to ministers, parties, governors and Congressmen. In congressional hearings, think tanks present their policy reforms and influence current legislation. Furthermore, former think tank scholars serve in high-ranking government positions.[67] Their political expertise and recommendations achieve greater relevance in policymaking when these are broadly discussed in public.[68]

Unlike party foundations in Germany, political parties in the US do not educate the future generation of political leadership and do not develop their policy proposals. In the decentralised and fragmented political system in the USA, political parties increasingly lose their significance. Think tanks thus obtain immense possibilities to promote their values.[69] Though once neglected in the literature of American public policy, observers of American politics begin to question the extent to which think tanks have defined, shaped and at times implemented policy ideas.[70]

---

[66] Gehlen, Martin: Politikberatung in den USA. Der Einfluß der Think Tanks auf die amerikanische Sozialpolitik. Frankfurt a.M.2005, pp. 35 - 36.

[67] Ibid., pp. 34-36.

[68] Glaab, Manuela/ Metz, Almut: Politikberatung und Öffentlichkeit. In: Falk, Svenja (ed.): Handbuch Poltikberatung. Wiesbaden 2006, p. 161-172 (p. 167).

[69] Braml, Josef: Deutsche und amerikanische Think Tanks. Voraussetzungen für ihr Wirken. Wissenschaft und Frieden 2004 – 4: Think Tanks. In www.wissenschaft-und-frieden.de/seite.php?artikellId=0337, pp. 1-5 (p. 5).

[70] Abelson, Donald E: Think Tanks in the United States. In: Stone, Diane/ Denham, Andrew/ Garnett, Mark (eds.): Think Tanks Across Nations. A Comparative Approach. Manchester, Manchester University Press 1998, pp. 107 – 126, (p. 107).

In the twentieth century, all American presidents but Woodrow Wilson, have publicly endorsed a research institute throughout their presidency, even though scholars began to speculate about their influence in American politics as late as the 1980s. Though consent to policies stays with elected officials, governments regularly consult think tanks for advise and information. Their influence may be limited on the construction of the political agenda, the development of policy alternatives und the solution of societal problems through their ideas. In the end, elected officials are responsible for the selection and the application of new policy proposals. According to Diane Stone, the influence of think tanks is therefore diffuse, variable and barely to measure.[71]

The influence of think tanks on US foreign policy can be explained by the balance of powers in the US constitution and the resulting fragmentation of the policy-making process, by the revolving door from think tank scholars into government, by the lack of a civil service and by weak party discipline.[72] Furthermore, the political system of the United States rests upon divided government, while one party rules in the White House the other party dominates Congress.[73] Even though the White House cannot initiate laws in Congress one may ask if the administration can influence legislation by engaging think tanks to promote their reform proposals in order to gain the public opinion. After the Republican realignment in Congress in 1994 conservative think tanks were more often invited to congressional hearings and had more media coverage than their liberal counterparts.[74] That is why the thesis looks at the role of the neoconservatives if they are in control of the agenda and thus influence the decision-making process.[75]

The influence of think tanks is often measured by the number of book sales, by the number of media presence and by the number of congressional hearings where their scholars present their policy proposals. Opinion polls have shown that policy-makers in Washington D.C. appraise advocacy think tanks because their staff contributes to the political debate and directs the public's attention to pragmatic issues. These think tanks commonly pursue to alter the elites' opinion for implementing their medium- to long-term studies into law. Their

[71] Stone, Diane: Capturing the Political Imagination. Think Tanks and the Policy Process. London, Frank Cass 1996, p. 2-3.
[72] Katz, Richard S.: Politische Parteien in den Vereinigten Staaten. Fokus Amerika der Friedrich-Ebert-Stiftung Nr.7, Washington, DC 2007.
[73] Reinicke, Wolfgang H.: Lotsendienste für die Politik: Think Tanks – amerikanische Erfahrungen und Perspektiven für Deutschland. Gtersloh 1996, pp. 8-9.
[74] Braml, Josef: Politikberatung amerikanischer Think Tanks. In: Falk, Svenja (Hrsg. u.a.): Handbuch Poltikberatung. Wiesbaden 2006, pp. 563-575 (p. 573).
[75] Arin, Kubilay Yado: Die Rolle der Think Tanks in der US-Außenpolitik. Von Clinton zu Bush Jr. Wiesbaden, VS Springer 2013.

financial resources and the practical political expertise of their scholars reflect the ideological orientation and their programmatic breadth. In the centre of their research lies the ideological interpretation of their findings instead of academic standards what leads to their closeness to policy-makers.[76] As awarding authority, the political community places high value to their policy expertise for the reason that their recommendations are distributed to the public to put their adversaries under political pressure to end their opposition.[77]

Referring to Abelson, attempts to measure the political impact of think tanks are under methodological strain. In pluralist societies where there exist great media freedoms idea factories can convince both policy-makers and the public from their values and their expertise. To this end, institutes pursue to bring members of Congress, their donors and their media partners up-to-date by their studies and research findings. The Heritage Foundation and the American Enterprise Institute managed to become under Reagan the ideological headquarters of the Republican Party which was accompanied by a direct involvement in the conservative administration and the support of elitist corporate ambitions.[78]

In this context, the thesis examines the question how think tanks compete for political impact on US foreign policy toward unilateralist or multilateral approaches. A comparison of liberal to conservative administrations explains why Democrats are concerned on losing international good will through Republican isolationism and later unilateralism, whereby the United States misses the unique opportunity to establish a global system based on the rule of law. The Republicans do on the contrary fear e.g. that the inability to build a strong defense gives the Soviet Union and later rogue nations the chance to threaten the USA.[79]

Think tanks according to pluralists play in another league than interests groups. Nevertheless, pluralists must acknowledge that policymakers often have a vested interest in influencing the outcome of group competition. Rather than behaving as referees they select organisations that may advance their own agendas. Presidential candidates turn to a select group of think tanks that share their own beliefs, values, and political outlook. Like President Bush jr. who looked to AEI, PNAC and the Hoover Institution for political advise. Moreover, congress-

---

[76] Higgott, Richard/Stone, Diane: The Limits of Influence: Foreign Policy Think Tanks in Britain and the USA. Review of International Studies, Vol. 20, No.1 (Jan. 1994), pp. 15 –34 . In. www.jstor.org/stable/20097355 [July 31st, 2009].
[77] Glaab, Manuela/ Metz, Almut: Politikberatung und Öffentlichkeit. In: Falk, Svenja (ed.): Handbuch Poltikberatung. Wiesbaden 2006, p. 161-172 (p. 165).
[78] Abelson, Donald E.: A New Channel of Influence. American Think Tanks and the News Media. Queen's Quarterly 1992, 99 (4), pp. 849 - 872.
[79] Mead, Walter R.: Power, Terror, Peace and War. America's Grand Strategy in a World at Risk. New York 2004, S.3ff.

men - under the Gingrich administration - decided which think-tank scholar should testify before congressional committees at critical stages of the policy-making process.[80] That is how the foreign policy establishment, the think tank scholars and academia, interact in emerging issues on national security, human rights, civil liberties and unilateral or multilateral approaches in U.S Foreign Policy.[81] The rivalry between Capitol Hill and White House has led on both sides of Pennsylvania Avenue to an increase in staff members and in the demand for external expertise.[82]

[80] Abelson, Donald E.: Do Think Tanks Matter? Assessing the Impact of Public Policy Institutes. 2nd Edition. Montreal, McGill-Quenn's University Press 2009, p. 53.
[81] Abelson, Donald E. "What Were They Thinking? Think Tanks, the Bush Administration and U.S. Foreign Policy," in Inderjeet Parmar, Linda B. Miller and Mark Ledwidge (eds), New Directions in US Foreign Policy. London: Routledge, 2009: pp. 92-105.
[82] Braml, Josef: Politikberatung amerikanischer Think Tanks. In: Falk, Svenja (ed..): Handbuch Poltikberatung. Wiesbaden 2006, pp. 563-575 (p. 565).

Fragmentation of the Political System and Veto Players

The political system of the USA is characterised by American exceptionalism. The United States cannot be understood without her founding myth of a chosen people. The American nation manifests itself in religious and moral terms. The religious notion is reaffirmed by evoking the Old Testament a nation under God, whereas the moral justification is brought forward to ascertain that the American nation embodies the Good in the world.[83] In Winthorp's words, "a city on a hill", emanates from the widely believed American civic religion that the United States is founded in a covenant with God.[84]

Particularly in the American literature it is frequently assumed that think tanks are unique to the US political system. The American historian, James Smith, for instance, has described think tanks as unique American policy-planning institutions, operating on the margins of the nation's political process.[85] His explanation of the proliferation of think tanks in the USA frequently points to the exceptional characteristics of the American political system. Smith argues that think tanks, bloom according to the political milieu in which they grow. Their presence on the unique scale found in the US is said to reflect America's constitutional separation of powers, the bicameral legislature, a party system historically grounded in electoral political ambitions rather than ideology and a civil service tradition that gives leeway to numerous political appointees.[86]

At the beginning of the twentieth century think tanks pursued the enlightenment of the American nation and its decision-makers without concern for their personal advantage. In their political advise to industry and media these institutes saved their clients' time for more important tasks. With their degrees in

---

[83] Haller, Gert: Die Bedeutung von Freiheit und Sicherheit in Europa und den USA. APuZ, 5-6/2008, pp. 9-14 (p. 10).

[84] Skillen, James W.: With or Against the World? America's Role Among the Nations. Lanham 2005, p. 15.

[85] Smith, James A.: The Idea Broker: Think Tanks and the Rise of the New Policy Elite. New York, Free Press 1991, p. XII.

[86] Ibid., p. XV.

social sciences, their technical and methodological abilities and their experience in public service the scholars guaranteed expertise, professionalism and intellect.[87] There are, however, doubts concerning the networks between politicians, journalists, managers and experts. In this view, political scientists perceive the danger that these networks misuse their political influence and their scholarly credibility to realise special interests of their donors disregarding the public interest. According to David Newsom, think tanks represent one of many types of organisations that populate the policy-making community. In terms of the American pluralist system, think tanks like interest groups, trade unions, environmental organisations and other NGOs compete among themselves for the attention of the policymakers. Since the government is regarded simply as moderator or referee overseeing the competition between NGOs, pluralists devote little attention to assessing government priorities. They view public policy not as a reflection of a specific government mandate but rather as an outcome of group competition to shape public policy.[88]

Diane Stone thus defines think tanks "as relatively autonomous organisations that are engaged in the analysis of policy issues, independently of government, political parties and pressure groups". [89] Think tanks are often financially dependent on these donors. Funding may come from government sources but these institutes are bound to keep their research freedom and are legally obliged to reject any specific interest. Through intellectual analysis policymaking is influenced and informed rather than direct lobbying. Rigorous analyses of policy issues are connected to their ideas and concepts. Towards, this end, think tanks repackage and generate information often directed to politicians or bureaucrats, but also to the media, interest groups, corporate leaders, and civil society.

Commenting on the fragmentation of the policymaking process, James Smith suggests that Woodrow Wilson's feared notion of a government of experts has come to pass. Smith contends that Wilson believed that democracy depended on the dedicated amateur who understood the concrete applications of a policy initiative and who could speak the language of the citizen. What we have now, according to Smith, is a tyranny of policy elites that has made American politics

---

[87] Stone, Diane: Capturing the Political Imagination. Think Tanks and the Policy Process. London, Frank Cass 1996, p. 16.
[88] Newsom, David D.: The Public Dimension of Foreign Policy. Bloomington, Indiana University Press 1996, pp. 141-162.
[89] Stone. Diane: Introduction. Think Tanks, Policy Advice, and Governance. In: Stone, Diane/ Denham, Andrew (eds.): Think Tank Traditions, Policy Research, and the Politics of Ideas. Manchester, Manchester University Press 2004, pp. 1-16 (pp. 1-2).

more polarised, short-sighted and fragmented. Their endless policy disputes leave aware citizens in frustration with the war of ideas.[90]

> „Emphasis will be placed on evaluating the various internal and external constraints that might limit the involvement of American think tanks in policy-making, as well as the incentives decision makers might have to turn to think tanks for policy advice. Particular emphasis will be placed on how think tanks are relying increasingly on the media to shape the political dialogue and what some of the implications of this strategy are."[91]

As Weaver points out weak and relatively non-ideological parties have enhanced think tanks' role in several ways. The most important feature of the US party system is that political parties have not themselves taken a major role in policy development by establishing sizeable policy research arms of their own. Think tanks have helped to fill this void by providing members of Congress and the executive with sound policy advise.[92] In the case of first- generation think tanks, their funding serves long-term research programs to attract more attention to social problems in the academic community, though their preferred target audience is policy-makers. Such think tanks like Brookings and CFR function in Kent Weaver's words much like universities without students.[93]

Veto players according to George Tsebelis are „individual or collective actors whose agreement is necessary for a change of status quo". An individual actor can be the president and a collective actor the Congress whereby veto players are distinguished through institutional or political affiliation. The political system in the USA assigns the Congress a predominant role as veto player. Veto players are all actors that are able to stop the implementation of policy reforms. Control of the agenda enables veto players, e.g. think tanks, corporations or the military, to change policy decisions to their benefit by pressuring elected officials which may damage the political system as a whole.[94]

A better understanding of foreign policy think tanks requires an examination of their activities and their experts' concepts. The approaches of policy communities, the epistemic communities, the advocacy coalitions, the policy entrepreneurs and network theories enable the observer to recognise the complete picture of the complex activities and motives of think tanks. These institutes play

[90] Smith, James A.: The Idea Brokers. Think-Tanks and the Rise of the New Policy Elite. New York, Free Press 1991, pp. 237-239.
[91] Abelson, Donald E.: Do Think Tanks Matter? Assessing the Impact of Public Policy Institutes. 2.Edition, Montreal, McGill-Queen's University Press 2009, p. 15.
[92] Weaver, R. Kent: The Changing World of Think Tanks. PS: Political Science and Politics. September 1989, pp. 563 – 578 (p. 570).
[93] Ibid., p. 566.
[94] Tsebelis, George: Veto Players. How Political Institutions Work. Princeton, Princeton University Press 2002.

an important role as platforms for discussions. With their ideas they generate the debate and contribute medium to long-term problem solutions.[95] The consensus in the political spectrum results according to John Kingdon rather from bargaining and negotiations than from persuasion for political support. The elected officials obtain in exchange for their support in the implementation of policy proposals concessions, compromises and provisions. Bargaining a law requires the abandonment of initial positions for achieving a sustainable majority in Congress.[96]

    For many think tanks, their proximity to Congress offers a direct bond to the American electorate, and the exertion of influence on public opinion and on politics.[97] "The apparently weak influence of the public will presumably disappoint those adherents of democratic theory"[98]. According to James Madison, one of the authors of the Federalist Papers, the constitutional separation of powers should constrain lobbies without popular mandate to obtain control over the nation's agenda.[99] Did the organised interests of the US economy influence US foreign policy to their own benefit with the aid of think tanks in the twentieth century?[100] The American citizen justifiably asks: who rules the nation?[101] Policy is mostly dictated by financially strong think tanks at the costs of politically and economically weaker non-governmental organisations.[102]

    Institutionalists, however, point out that outsiders can easily determine the author of an idea on the political agenda, in doing so they will find neither an ideological competition nor an image of elitist interests. Instead, there exists an

---

[95] Stone, Diane: Introduction: Think Tanks, Policy Advice, and Governance. In: Stone, Diane/ Denham, Andrew (eds.): Think Tank Traditions. Policy Research and the Politics of Ideas. Manchester, Manchester University Press 2004, pp. 1-16 (pp. 10-11).

[96] Kingdon, John W.: Agendas, Alternatives and Public Policies. Boston, Little, Brown & Company, 1984, p. 208.

[97] Ricci, David M: The Transformation of American Politics. The New Washington and the Rise of Think Tanks. New Haven, Yale University Press, 1993, p. 164.

[98] Jacobs, Lawrence R./ Page, Benjamin I.: Who Influences U.S. Foreign Policy? The American Political Science Review, Vol. 99, No. 1 (Febr. 2005); pp. 107 – 123 (p. 121). In: www. jstor.org/stable/30038922 [July 31st, 2009].

[99] Abelson, Donald E.: A Capitol Idea. Think Tanks and U.S. Foreign Policy. Montreal 2006, p. 110.

[100] Higgott, Richard/Stone, Diane: The Limits of Influence: Foreign Policy Think Tanks in Britain and the USA. Review of International Studies, Vol. 20, No.1 (Jan. 1994), pp 15 –34 (p. 17). In. www.jstor.org/stable/20097355.

[101] Glaab, Manuela/ Metz, Almut: Politikberatung und Öffentlichkeit. In: Falk, Svenja (ed..): Handbuch Poltikberatung. Wiesbaden 2006, pp. 161-172 (p. 169).

[102] Vgl. Higgott, Richard/Stone, Diane: The Limits of Influence: Foreign Policy Think Tanks in Britain and the USA. Review of International Studies, Vol. 20, No.1 (Jan. 1994), pp. 15 –34 . In. www.jstor.org/stable/20097355.

informed dialogue between independent and neutral policy experts.[103] Indeed, there can be no doubt that think tanks place like corporations a higher value on their benefit than on the public interest. Nevertheless, they play a key role in the consultation of politicians and the education of the public.[104] Yet, both in American politics and in the public, mistrust in experts increases because their opinions are widely believed to contain ideological motives.[105]

While McGann blames the short-term orientation of elected officials and weak party unity for the fragmentation of the policy formulation process. Think tanks thus are more a symptom than the problem itself. Although, they complicate the political process, eliminating them in order to limit debate and innovation would be ineffective as well as undesirable. Think tanks are simply responding to the chaos that exists in the political environment, and while they may add to it, they are not responsible. In a pluralistic society, where power is decentralised and political parties are weak, policy research organisations and other interest groups play a positive and stabilising role in the political process.[106]

There exists a link between the weakening of parties and of their ability to develop policy and the emergence of independent groups or institutes – often associated with particular leaders or tendencies within parties – to assume the agenda-setting role which mass parties once claimed to perform. Pressure groups in democratic systems establish policy institutes to lend added weight to the arguments they wish to make – and to take advantage of tax exempt status of research organisations from campaign activities or overt lobbying. Political parties similarly use formal autonomous institutes (DLC, PPI) which do not immediately commit the party leadership or to conduct internal debates among different tendencies.[107] Through the participation of prominent policymakers in their seminars and conferences, and the collaboration as presidential advisers, in congressional committees, and in transition teams think tanks play a decisive role in political decision-making.[108] Because of the weak party system in the US, a po-

---

[103] McGann, James G.: The Competition for Dollars, Scholars and Influence in the Public Policy Research Industry . Lanham, University Press of America, 1995, p. 106.

[104] Ibd., p. 96.

[105] Gehlen, Martin: Kulturen der Politkberatung – USA. In: Bröchler, Stephan/ Schützeichel, Rainer eds.): Politikberatung. Stuttgart 2008, pp. 480 – 492 (p. 486).

[106] McGann, James G.: The Competition for Dollars, Scholars and Influence in the Public Policy Research Industry . Lanham, University Press of America, 1995, p. 44.

[107] Wallace, William: Conclusion. Ideas and Influence. In: Stone, Diane/ Denham, Andrew/ Garnett, Mark (Eds.): Think Tanks Across Nations. Manchester, Manchester University Press 1998, pp. 223-230, (p. 226).

[108] Reinicke, Wolfgang H.: Lotsendienste für die Politik: Think Tanks – amerikanische Erfahrungen und Perspektiven für Deutschland. Gütersloh 1996, p. 39 and pp. 46-47.

litical system, that encourages members of Congress to pursue the interests of their voters and that of lobbies instead of the party line, deputies need not fear that closeness to a certain think tank and its ideas could undermine party unity.[109]

The number of conservative think tanks doubles those of liberal institutes. As part of a conservative infrastructure of foundations, managers, journalists, and policy-makers, research institutes promote ideas like tradition, family values and the deregulated free market. Republicans preserved their preeminence in the war of ideas thanks to support from right-wing think tanks.[110] Political battles are more important than consensus and compromise in decision-making. Congress is divided on partisan lines[111] no side will give in leading to a deadlock in policy innovations.[112] Under such circumstances, think tanks become passionate advocates of an ideological policy that shows no readiness to a ba-lanced debate where competing ideas can be examined.[113]

Dominated classed internalise these conceptions which are generated within an array of civil society institutions. Social revolution involves breaking with the ideological hegemony, creating a new culture and a new view of humanity and society that can win the active support of the masses of people.[114] For these reasons, neoconservative intellectuals called for a reassertion of state authority and a reduction in social welfare expenditures and business regulations on the home front.[115] Power in Congress should be centralized, the presidency strengthened, and the political parties reinvigorated.[116] This reflects the values of 'order' and 'stability' that set limits on the range of imaginable outcomes.[117]

---

[109] Higgott, Richard/Stone, Diane: The Limits of Influence: Foreign Policy Think Tanks in Britain and the USA. Review of International Studies, Vol. 20, No.1 (Jan. 1994), pp. 15 –34 (p.33). In. www.jstor.org/stable/20097355 [July 31st, 2009].

[110] Rich, Andrew: The War of Ideas. In: Kazin, Michael/ Becker, Frans/ Hurenkamp, Menno (eds.): In Search of Progressive America. Philadelphia, University of Pennsylvania Press, pp. 73 –84 (p. 73).

[111] "While policy advocates cannot ensure the stable rule of the interests they represent, they can and helped direct debate away from capitalism and toward the alleged excesses of democratic aspiration by the New Left as a source of crisis. As the crisis of the 1970s unfolded, elites saw the expansion of liberal democracy as endangering the social order and the economic system they presided over." Peschek, Joseph G.: Policy-Planning Organisations. Elite Agendas and America's Rightward Turn. Philadelphia, Temple University Press 1987, p. 241

[112] Ibd., p. 90.

[113] Laipson, Ellen (Präsident und CEO): The Henry L. Stimson Center. In: McGann, James G.: Think Tanks and Policy Advice in the United States: Academics, Advisors and Advocates. New York, Routledge 2007, pp. 94 – 97 (p. 95).

[114] Peschek, Joseph G.: Policy-Planning Organisations. Elite Agendas and America's Rightward Turn. Philadelphia, Temple University Press 1987, p. 229.

[115] Ibid., pp. 40- 41.

[116] Ibid., p. 209.

[117] Ibid, p. 241.

CFR, Brookings and the Neoconservative Advocacy Think Tanks

Brookings, CFR and Carnegie Endowment trace their origins back to the early twentieth century and the progressive good-government movement. Their goal is to improve government performance, reduce corruption and bossism, and perfect the practice of American democracy.[118] Universities without students are composed of dozens of academics hired to write scholarly studies, to assume teaching, and administrative responsibilities. They function like universities in the sense that their principal mission is to promote a greater understanding of important social, economic and political issues confronting society. Unlike universities, however, the seminars and workshops they offer and the studies they produce are generally intended for policy-makers not students.[119]

America's oldest and most revered think tanks Brookings and CFR have cultivated a reputation as independent institutes, that assign the highest priority to providing objective research and neutral, intellectually independent analysis.[120] Early research institutes offered political leaders vital assistance in charting the new course for America's future. By engaging in policy research instead of political advocacy, early twentieth-century think tanks helped foster close and lasting ties to policy-makers. While these institutions attracted policy experts committed to a wide range of political beliefs, the organisations themselves were rarely transformed into ideological battlefields.[121]

Individual scholars at times overtly supposed or opposed governmental policies, but their primary goal and that of their institutions was not to impose their political agenda on policy-makers but to improve and help rationalize the decision-making process. Since these institutions did not solicit and rarely received government funding, they could criticise government policy without

---

[118] Wiarda, Howard: Conservative Brain Trust. The Rise, Fall, and Rise Again of the American Enterprise Institute. Lanham, Lexington Books, 2009, pp.3- 4.

[119] Abelson, Donald E.: Do Think Tanks Matter? Assessing the Impact of Public Policy Institutes. 2nd Edition. Montreal, McGill-Queen's University Press 2009,pp. 18-19.

[120] Ibid., p. 23

[121] Abelson, Donald E: Think Tanks in the United States. In: Stone, Diane/ Denham, Andrew/ Garnett, Mark (eds.): Think Tanks Across Nations. A Comparative Approach. Manchester, Manchester University Press 1998, pp. 107 – 126, (p. 111).

jeopardising their million-dollar endowments from philantrops such as Carnegie, Rockefeller or Ford. Policy research institutes, in Abelson's opinion, are less vulnerable to the partisan pressures of donors and for the most part, early think tanks are committed to scholarly research.[122] The CFR had prepared the institutional framework of the Bretton Woods System of IMF, World Bank and GATT to help member nations to overcome temporary trade deficits and to make loans to help finance the postwar recovery.[123] While the US had lowered tariffs on European imports to remove obstacles to European recovery and come to its financial aid though the Marshall Plan, the Europeans, with US assent, continued to maintain some obstacles to US goods. When in America's national security the recovery of war-torn economies provided markets for US exports, financial aid was made to stop Communist parties from gaining elections.[124] America's global economic thrust rested on the political foundations of the Bretton-Woods-System and the security networks made possible by US hegemony.[125] The US dollar became the principal world reserve currency.[126]

The Brookings alliance of business and scholars espousing free trade and administered reform had presented the dominant ideas of the post-1945 American political economy: Keynesianism. As its leaders' institutional affiliations with the Council of Economic Advisers suggested, the Brookings Institution has been associated with the liberal internationalist wing of American establishment. But the conservative challenges of the 1970's onwards were reflected in recent Brookings' activity. New concerns with monetary policy, capital formation, deregulation, and Soviet policy were brought about by the New Right. With the impact of the economic crisis on the mainstream of liberal democratic capitalist thought, a once-confident Brookings Keynesianism was in retreat.[127]

As long as the economy produced growth and relative prosperity, the Bretton Woods system was not called into question. Stagflation of the 1970s and 1980s politicised economic policy in the U.S. Free-marketers desired a reduction in government, subsidies for American industries and tariffs on imported goods from Europe and Japan.[128] In the US during the 1970s and 1980s, the politics of business (elite mobilisation) has been caused principally by economic declining situation and the political opposition of labor unions. The international economic

---

[122] Ibid.,. p. 111.
[123] Peschek, Joseph G.: Policy-Planning Organisations. Elite Agendas and America's Rightward Turn. Philadelphia, Temple University Press 1987, p. 42.
[124] Ibid, pp. 40-49.
[125] Ibid, p. 72.
[126] Ibid, p. 43.
[127] Abelson, Donald E.: American Think-Tanks and their Role In US Foreign Policy. London, MacMillan Press Ltd. 1996, pp. 21- 23.
[128] Ibid, p. 49.

crisis led to foreign-policy disarray and economic downturn. The political system in the USA was unable to devise greater coherence in problem-definition, imperatives, and formulation of policy recommendations, i.e. a political strategy for economic recovery.[129] Supported in large part by donors from foundations, corporations and philanthropists, scholars at institutions like Brookings regard book-length studies as their primary research products.[130] Both the Brookings Institution and the Heritage Foundation conduct research and to varying degrees market their findings. The main difference is in the emphasis they place on pure research and political advocacy. To argue that Brookings is a policy research institution and that Heritage is an advocacy think tank, would be superficial. Referring to Brookings as a world-renowned policy research institution provides the organization with instant credibility producing objective and balanced research. Conversely, as a well-known advocacy think tank, Heritage must be more committed to furthering its ideology than to pursuing scholarly research. As a result, the views and recommendations of "research institutions" should be taken more seriously than those of "advocacy think tanks". Classifying think tanks incorrectly may stem from these organizations' similar strategies to convey their ideas. Think tanks frequently alter their behavior to become more competitive in the marketplace of ideas.[131] Despite portraying itself as scholarly institution, Brookings devotes considerable resources to advocacy. Brookings has been criticised for its partisan (centrist) leanings. In part, this is based on contributions its scholars have made supporting particular presidential candidates.[132]

As advocacy think tanks emerged in the 1970s, scholars realised that developing effective marketing techniques to enhance their status in the policy-making community rather than providing policy-makers with sound and impartial advise had become their main priority which had the implication of the politicisation of policy expertise. After a period of sustained economic growth from 1945-70, the US enforced its nationalist economic policies on the Bretton-Woods-System. Simultaneous inflation and high unemployment (stagflation) wrecked the US economy, a shaky debt structure threatened corporate and financial interests with bankruptcy, and the growing gaps between government revenues and expenditures led to concern about a fiscal crisis of the state.[133] Brookings and AEI emerged as rivals in the 1950s and 1960s debating the merits of

---

[129] Ibid, pp. 66-67.
[130] Abelson, Donald E.: Do Think Tanks Matter? Assessing the Impact of Public Policy Institutes. 2nd Edition. Montreal, McGill-Queen's University Press 2009, p. 18-19.
[131] Ibid., p. 21.
[132] Ibid., p. 282.
[133] Peschek, Joseph G.: Policy-Planning Organisations. Elite Agendas and America's Rightward Turn. Philadelphia, Temple University Press 1987 pp. 40- 49.

Keynes versus more traditional market economics, and then clashed over again on Lyndon B. Johnson's Great Society programs. With the advancement of Heritage, the polarisation and ideological conflict of American society became greater. Brookings was positioned on the moderate left, CSIS in the middle and AEI on the moderate right, whereas the Heritage Foundation was placed on the far right according to Howard Wiarda.[134]

As the 1970's moved on the free-market, business-friendly ideology of the neoconservatives discredited liberal Keynesian economic policy-positions, meshed with foreign policy hardliners.[135] Since the 1970s, the most common type of think tank to emerge has been what Weaver terms as the advocacy think tank. Advocacy think tanks as the name suggests combine a strong policy, partisan or ideological bent with aggressive salesmanship in an effort to influence current policy debates.[136] The war of ideas was waged by AEI and Heritage since the mid-1970s to challenge the Brookings Institution for the title of Washington's leading think tank on economic and domestic issues.[137]

The Council on Foreign Relations was still aligned with multinational capital and saw the major threat to US hegemony as divisions within the capitalist world and economic nationalism in the Third World. The liberal foreign policy establishment advocated greater collaboration among the advanced powers, concessions on North-South-trade, and the pursuit of détente with the USSR.[138] But the decline of American hegemony meant that American goods were losing competition to Japanese and European imports, large parts of the Third World sought independence from US economic and military control, e.g. the oil-weapon of OPEC. The dollar was twice devalued. Nixon suspended the conversion of dollars into gold to improve the trade and payments balances of the US. Negative trade balances led to protectionist pressures from US manufacturing industries. Disregarding GATT regulations Nixon imposed a 10% surcharge on most imports to the US. Japan and Western Europe agreed to loosen trade restrictions on US imports.[139]

A reordering of world political economy as demanded by CFR and Brookings aroused domestic opposition from AEI and Heritage, which feared a

---

[134] Wiarda, Howard: Conservative Brain Trust. The Rise, Fall, and Rise Again of the American Enterprise Institute. Lanham, Lexington Books, 2009, pp.3- 4.
[135] Peschek, Joseph G.: Policy-Planning Organisations. Elite Agendas and America's Right-Ward Turn. Philadelphia, Temple University Press 1987, pp. 35- 37.
[136] Weaver, R. Kent: Changing the World of Think Tanks. Political Science p. 567
[137] Peschek, Joseph G.: Policy-Planning Organisations. Elite Agendas and America's Right-Ward Turn. Philadelphia, Temple University Press 1987, pp. 27- 34.
[138] Ibid pp. 16-17.
[139] Abelson, Donald E.: American Think-Tanks and their Role In US Foreign Policy. London, MacMillan Press Ltd. 1996, pp. 40-49.

loss of power as policy decisions were relocated to international institutions.[140] During the 1960s and 70s, AEI emerged as the great conservative counterbalance to the Brookings Institution. For the last decades, the debate between these two institutions and their scholars largely set the parameters of US economic policy. Brookings was liberal, Keynesian, and closely tied to the Democratic Party. Many of its economists had been in charge of the wartime controls on US economy that AEI had railed against. AEI was in contrast free market oriented. Its lodestar was not Keynes but Milton Friedman. AEI stood for unfettered capitalism against communism and government interference in economy. AEI was widely viewed as mouthpiece for big business, a trade association. Not surprisingly, AEI supported the 1964 Goldwater's, then Nixon's and later Reagan's presidential campaigns.[141]

In 1977, Jimmy Carter came into office with a program of military spending cutbacks, human rights, a conciliatory approach to the USSR, and international policy coordination among allies. Carter's purpose was undoubtedly to regain the moral high ground for the US. With the Cold War subsiding, a newly confident US could shape a foreign policy above narrow national interests, look for solutions to threat of nuclear war, racial hatred, the arms race, environmental damage, hunger and disease. By 1980, turmoil in the developing world, the Iranian revolution, continued dependence of the democracies on imported Middle Eastern oil and at the top the Soviet military invasion in Afghanistan led to a hardening militarist retrenchment in US foreign policy. Inside the US an elite-level conflict over the direction of foreign policy was pushing Carter to the right.[142]

Carter's foreign policy united all of the diverse scholars at AEI. In elevating human rights abuse above other foreign policy values and interests meanwhile reducing the Pentagon undermining the CIA, and denigrating traditional national interest and balance of power politics he violated every principle of realism. He criticised human rights abuses of friendly regimes in Asia, the Middle East, Africa and Latin America. Public opinion in Iran, Nicaragua, Argentina, Brazil, and El Salvador turned against the US. While damaging economic, diplomatic, political and military interests, the US was in danger of losing the Cold War.[143]

---

[140] Ibid, p. 72-73.
[141] Wiarda, Howard: Conservative Brain Trust. The Rise, Fall, and Rise Again of the American Enterprise Institute. Lanham, Lexington Books, 2009, pp.5- 6.
[142] Peschek, Joseph G.: Policy-Planning Organisations. Elite Agendas and America's Rightward Turn. Philadelphia, Temple University Press 1987, p. 107-109.
[143] Wiarda, Howard: Conservative Brain Trust. The Rise, Fall, and Rise Again of the American Enterprise Institute. Lanham, Lexington Books, 2009, p.8

Liberal claims for reforming the international economic system met the opposition of Heritage and AEI. Their donors in the business world believed that the risks outweighed the likely benefits of plans that would involve greater state commitments or substantial changes in the organisation of the international economy.[144] For the AEI neoconservatives, a positive view of American democratic capitalism had to be rekindled to win support for a decisive foreign policy. Therefore, the Neocons tried to discredit domestic critics and encourage capitalist extension abroad.[145] Increased prosperity should divert attention from the structure of power in society and driving forces in economy.[146] Privatisation, deregulation, government downsizing, monetarist supply-side economics were put into effect by Reagan.[147]

The AEI and Heritage did not, in general, take the growing interdependence of the international economy, and the US role in globalization, as the touchstone of America's economic policy. While systemic liberalization is a goal and some policy coordination desirable, their agenda focuses on restoring growth and profitability to the national economy through conservative, pro-business deregulation and limited government whose benefits spill over into the global arena. By contrast, the CFR and Brookings scholars begin with the processes of the world economy, under which are subsumed the prospects for national political economies.[148] Like the AEI, the Heritage Foundation saw the route to international economic adjustment as based on domestic revitalisation to be achieved by free markets. Barriers to foreign trade and investments are to be removed by developing countries, export subsidies abolished and import curbs resisted.[149]

Heritage and AEI were also persistent critics of foreign aid programs and of many measures that would increase the resources of the IMF or the World Bank. Third-World countries should adopt free-market measures, reduce their state sector, and open their economies to the free flow of private foreign capital. The Heritage approach thus required no messy new levels of policy coordination or institution building. It fitted nicely in with the unilateralism of the American

---

[144] Peschek, Joseph G.: Policy-Planning Organisations. Elite Agendas and America's Rightward Turn. Philadelphia, Temple University Press 1987, p. 77.
[145] Abelson, Donald E.: American Think-Tanks and their Role In US Foreign Policy. London, MacMillan Press Ltd. 1996,, p. 152.
[146] Ibid, p. 241.
[147] Wiarda, Howard: Conservative Brain Trust. The Rise, Fall, and Rise Again of the American Enterprise Institute. Lanham, Lexington Books, 2009, pp.5- 6.
[148] Peschek, Joseph G.: Policy-Planning Organisations. Elite Agendas and America's Rightward Turn. Philadelphia, Temple University Press 1987, p. 93.
[149] Abelson, Donald E.: American Think-Tanks and their Role In US Foreign Policy. London, MacMillan Press Ltd. 1996, p. 150.

right. [150] Before the politicisation of foreign policy caused by the Vietnam War, the State Department could carry out policy largely insulated from domestic political pressures. [151] Standing in opposition to the liberal CFR and gaining strength under Carter and Reagan was a bloc of military officers, intelligence operatives, Cold War intellectuals, arms producers organized in the Committee on Present Danger. They saw Third World turmoil as a result of Soviet expansionism, challenging US hegemony that had to be confronted with a strong military build-up of conventional and nuclear forces. [152] Carter's critics in the State Department, Pentagon and CIA, influenced by realist positions claimed that Carter had alienated important regional friends and allies such as Chile, Indonesia, Philippines, South Korea, Taiwan and South Africa. Meanwhile, the democratic president was ignoring the immense military build-up and threat posed by the Soviet Union. [153] Military capabilities were in their view in danger of becoming inferior because of the crisis of the political spirit, cultural and moral disarray. [154]

In those days, a major gravitation to the right had been occurring among American intellectuals who were called "neoconservatives" and then constituted the major intellectual current at AEI. Disillusioned by the Great Society Programs, the anti-Vietnam protests by the Left, these neocons hold strong reservations on Carter, were worried about the Soviet-Arab threat to Israel's existence and thus attracted to Reagan's Republican administration. [155] By the 1980s foreign policy had become as much politicised as domestic policy was. [156] Even though criticising Carter for his failed human rights policy, Howard Wiarda, a former Reagan advisor on Latin America, concludes that a multi-pronged approach - democracy, human rights, development, military reform, diplomacy, US pressure and security - is necessary for policy success in Congress, building consensus over partisan, ideological lines. [157]

---

[150] Ibid.

[151] Wiarda, Howard: Conservative Brain Trust. The Rise, Fall, and Rise Again of the American Enterprise Institute. Lanham, Lexington Books, 2009 p. 123.

[152] Peschek, Joseph G.: Policy-Planning Organisations. Elite Agendas and America's Rightward Turn. Philadelphia, Temple University Press 1987, pp. 16-17.

[153] Irving Kristol, Nathan Glazer, Norman Podhoeretz, Daniel Patrick Moynihan, Seymour Martin Lipset, Daniel Bell, Samuel Huntington, Keane Kirkpatrick and Michael Novak were all Neocons according to Wiarda, Howard: Conservative Brain Trust. The Rise, Fall and Rise Again of the American Enterprise Institute. Lanham, Lexington Books, 2009, p.9.

[154] Peschek, Joseph G.: Policy-Planning Organisations. Elite Agendas and America's Rightward Turn. Philadelphia, Temple University Press 1987, p. 128.

[155] Wiarda, Howard: Conservative Brain Trust. The Rise, Fall, and Rise Again of the American Enterprise Institute. Lanham, Lexington Books, 2009, p. 10.

[156] Ibid, p. 123.

[157] Ibid, p. 129.

Reagan's and Carter's mandate was no less than the democratisation of the globe. That included aid to both anti-authoritarian and anticommunist groups. It also included technical assistance to help new democracies run elections, develop free markets, build political parties, and civil society, fashion pluralism. It goes without saying that all the groups were supposed to be pro-American and anticommunist.[158] Howard Wiarda draws the conclusion that America had never been able to function with a Kissingeresque, strictly realist foreign policy. Rather America and American foreign policy have always functioned best when they were able to reconcile hard-headed realism and pragmatism with idealist democracy and human rights concerns. The neocons at AEI stood ready to provide both toughness and political savvy in the spotlight on democracy and human rights in the American body politic.[159]

Heritage released a massive blueprint for the conservative Reagan administration called Mandate for Leadership.[160] Unlike earlier types of think tanks, the Heritage Foundation elevated political advocacy to its primary purpose. The founders of advocacy think tanks were determined to market their ideas in the political arena, the policymakers, the public, and the media. In quick-response policy research, Heritage emphasised the need to provide members of Congress and the executive with one-to-two page briefing notes on key domestic and foreign policy issues. It also stressed the importance of marketing its ideas to the media.[161] Previously on the fringes of national political discussion, the neocons were able to wield clout under the Reagan administration. Hard-line organisations of the New Right competed with a center that had itself become more conservative, enjoying the support of the forces that swept Ronald Reagan into power.[162]

Its study Mandate for Leadership was widely circulated in Washington and was frequently cited in the media. Heritage later claimed that more than 60% of its proposals had been adopted by the Reagan administration.[163] Confronting secularism at home and abroad offered opportunities for winning moral and political battles in the American political culture. The drive for hard power formed part, for AEI thinkers, of reordering US foreign policy, combining increased

---

[158] Ibid, p.105.
[159] Wiarda, Howard: Conservative Brain Trust. The Rise, Fall, and Rise Again of the American Enterprise Institute. Lanham, Lexington Books, 2009 p. 310.
[160] Peschek, Joseph G.: Policy-Planning Organisations. Elite Agendas and America's Rightward Turn. Philadelphia, Temple University Press 1987, p. 32.
[161] Abelson, Donald E.: Do Think Tanks Matter? Assessing the Impact of Public Policy Institutes. 2nd Edition. Montreal, McGill-Quenn's University Press 2009, p. 31-32.
[162] Peschek, Joseph G.: Policy-Planning Organisations. Elite Agendas and America's Rightward Turn. Philadelphia, Temple University Press 1987, pp. 27- 34.
[163] Ibid, p. 32.

defense spending with interventionism in the Third World. The AEI favoured a foreign policy based on free trade coupled with arms race against the USSR.[164] Low intensity conflict, and unconventional CIA sponsored anti-Marxist insurgencies should roll back radical regimes in the Third World, these determinants of the Reagan Doctrine were masterminded by Heritage. The "militarist" neocons organized around an America besieged were ready to recoup their rightful place in the world under strong leadership. This political shift was made possible by increased budgets of leading conservative policy-planning organization AEI and Heritage. No longer were Brookings and CFR without serious competition. But there was no reason to believe that the militarist faction would be more successful in forging a world order, though the climate it helped to create was fraught with danger.[165] With the exception of Frank Carlucci and Colin Powell, none of Reagan's National Security Advisers could be considered impressive or heavy weights in the tradition of Henry Kissinger and Zbigniew Brzesinski. According to Wiarda, the NSC under Reagan was incompetent and the worst functioning NSC since its creation in 1947.[166]

Under Reagan, US foreign policy was defined in national security terms revealing a decline of centrist decisions and a militarisation of strategic thinking that stressed anti-communism and military readiness with deep skepticism about arms control with the USSR. The AEI and Heritage replaced CFR and Brookings.[167] Moreover, foreign policy was increasingly dominated by domestic political considerations not a measured weighing of non-partisan rational interests. Almost all interest groups, public opinion parties, the Congress, the media, even think tanks reflected these divisions and reinforced it. Wiarda saw the American political system since Vietnam and Watergate as fragmented, divided and polarised.[168]

As an advisor to the Reagan administration Wiarda observed during the Reagan years the blockade that prevailed in Washington D.C. Congress, on the one hand, was dominated by partisanship, political log-rolling, and concern for its members' reelection bids that it lost its role in foreign policy. On the other hand, Wiarda could not believe how conservative Reagan advisers engaged in growing party polarisation. It was hard to believe that the Reagan government

---

[164] Abelson, Donald E.: American Think-Tanks and their Role In US Foreign Policy. London, MacMillan Press Ltd. 1996, p. 152.

[165] Ibid, pp.160-162.

[166] Wiarda, Howard: Conservative Brain Trust. The Rise, Fall, and Rise Again of the American Enterprise Institute. Lanham, Lexington Books, 2009 p.39.

[167] Peschek, Joseph G.: Policy-Planning Organisations. Elite Agendas and America's Right-ward Turn. Philadelphia, Temple University Press 1987, p. 112- 113.

[168] Wiarda, Howard: Conservative Brain Trust. The Rise, Fall, and Rise Again of the American Enterprise Institute. Lanham, Lexington Books, 2009 p. 203.

operated on such an ideological, non-pragmatic, and ill-informed level.[169] As conservative foundations supported the Heritage Foundation and cut funding to AEI because these right-wing donors considered AEI too liberal, the AEI scholars looked for financial backing to Reverend Moon. Bad finances made the moderately conservative AEI to a right-wing think tank and a neoconservative bastion under Irving Kristol and Richard Perle in the mid-1980s.[170] Outlined on the right by Heritage, on the left by Brookings that itself shifted to the center as AEI moved to the right.[171] The neocons at AEI plotted and forced the moderates out, among them Howard Wiarda. Sidney Blumenthal, a liberal commentator at the Washington Post, blamed AEI not just for administrative mismanagement but also for abandoning its conservative base in favour of a centrist position.[172] Within the AEI, there were ideological and personal rivalries and bitter disputes on its future. In the midst of these political fights AEI verged on the edge of bankruptcy. Only in recent years with its neoconservatism and proximity to George W. Bush AEI has recovered both its finances and its policy influence. In Wiarda's observation, AEI is at the centre of policy formulation, speech-writing, budget analyses, political campaigning and policy advocacy.[173]

---

[169] Ibid, p. 185.
[170] Abelson, Donald E.: American Think-Tanks and their Role In US Foreign Policy. London, Mac-Millan Press Ltd. 1996, pp. 225-236.
[171] Ibid, p. 241.
[172] Ibid, pp. 256- 264.
[173] Ibid p. VIII.

Elite Theory

In the political system of the USA parties loose their importance in an increasingly decentralised and fragmented political environment.[174] Elite theorists, like Peschek, Domhoff and Dye, examine the role of think tanks and try to prove their political influence by the revolving door principle, by the participation of well-known politicians in their seminars and conferences, by their scholars' testimonies in congressional hearings, and their assistance in election campaigns.[175]

The elite theorist Peschek provided an analytical framework for the interconnectedness of policy-planning organisations with social and economic power in the USA. Their political function results from the historical development of research institutes in times of foreign policy change in the international system after both World Wars, the Cold War and the war on terror. Focusing on the ideological orientation of scholars and the political polarisation of American politics in the war of ideas, the right-ward turn can be deduced form the political activities of think tanks such as CFR, Brookings, PPI, AEI and Heritage Foundation.[176]

Think tanks seek to influence policy-makers in the corridors of power: serving on task forces and transition teams, maintaining liason offices with Congress, inviting policy-makers to conferences and seminars and workshops, offering help in fundraising campaigns through contact to large donors. The revolving door from research institute into high-level government and vice versa promotes the career of scholars or former politicians. Access to key politicians asserts think tanks' influence on current legislation by way of policy briefs for lawmakers.[177] Elite theorists Peschek, Dye and Domhoff have pointed out that

---

[174] Braml, Josef: Deutsche und amerikanische Think Tanks. Voraussetzungen für ihr Wirken. Wissenschaft und Frieden 2004 – 4: Think Tanks. In www.wissenschaft-und-frieden.de/seite.php?artikellId=0337, pp. 1-5 (p. 5).

[175] Reinicke, Wolfgang H.: Lotsendienste für die Politik: Think Tanks – amerikanische Erfahrungen und Perspektiven für Deutschland. Gütersloh 1996, p. 39 and pp. 46-47.

[176] Arin, Kubilay Yado: Die Rolle der Think Tanks in der US-Außenpolitik. Von Clinton zu Bush Jr. Wiesbaden, VS Springer 2013.

[177] Abelson, Donald E.: Do Think Tanks Matter? Assessing the Impact of Public Policy Institutes. 2nd Edition. Montreal, McGill-Queen's University Press 2009, p 120 – 121.

think tanks personate key actors in the American power elites. The power of decision-making is concentrated in the hands of a small group of corporate leaders,
policy-makers and opinion-makers. According to Stone and Garnett, the difficulty of elite theory consists in its one-sided focus on well-known institutes that
have lasting ties to political parties and the industry. Like elite theorists, neo-
marxists just refer to most prominent think tanks to prove that capitalist problems deserve state solutions. Thus the radical left contradicts conservative institutes and their donors who propagate deregulation. i.e. free markets without government interference. The capital, in Stone's and Garnett's view, pursues hegemonic projects to preserve its privileges and to obtain profits. In neo-marxist
classification of think tanks, these institutes serve as ruling instrument of the
capitalist classes whose leadership in media, politics, and economy are sworn in
to a common policy direction for shaping the public opinion to their benefit. [178]

Think tanks bestow on corporate interests the credibility of scientific research that generous donors require to get access to the media, to universities and
to key actors in politics and bureaucracy. Think tanks, in terms of elite theory,
use their contacts to implement the political and economic interests of their donors – the ruling class.[179] In this context, one must mention the military industrial complex or iron triangles that constitute a sworn-in community of academics, managers and former politicians, who appeal to officials for realising their
elitist agenda and for securing their financial interests: a political lobbyism that
is formally not allowed to bear this name though it enables one-time high-
ranking administration officials to write their biography.[180]

Think tanks serve as idea providers in the policy arena, as intermedia-
ries between universities and government, as providers of options to politicians,
as pools of talent to new administrations as well as "resting places" for out-of-
office politicians.[181] Particularly during presidential campaigns, think tanks are
portrayed as the architects of new and sometimes innovative agendas because of
their close ties to candidates. Think tanks are said to be responsible for the political and economic agendas of incoming administrations.[182] In short, think tanks

---

[178] Stone, Diane/ Garnett, Mark: Introduction: Think Tanks, Policy Advice and Governance. In.
Stone, Diane/ Denham, Andrew/ Garnett, Mark (eds): Think Tanks Across Nations. Manchester,
Manchester University Press 1998, pp. 1-20, (p. 13-14).
[179] Abelson, Donald E.: A Capitol Idea. Think Tanks and U.S. Foreign Policy. Montreal 2006, pp. 97-
99.
[180] Hennis, Michael: Der neue Militärisch-Industrielle Komplex in den USA. APuZ, B46/2003, pp.
41-46.
[181] Wiarda, Howard: Conservative Brain Trust. The Rise, Fall, and Rise Again of the American Enterprise Institute. Lanham, Lexington Books, 2009 p. 4.
[182] Abelson, Donald E./ Carberry, Christine M.: Policy Experts in Presidential Campaigns. A Model
of Think Tank Recruitment. Presidential Studies Quarterly, 1997, 27 (4), pp. 679 – 697.

have stepped into the vacuum created by the sheer bigness, bureaucracy and time-consuming procedure of government to provide a useful service to discuss the ideas and policies and make recommendations on the issues that most government officials and congressmen no longer have the time to study in depth. Think tanks provide the background, the history, the context that government officials cannot take the time to do.[183] That is why the Heritage Foundation is structured more like a newspaper than a university and is staffed almost exclusively by young professionals and less well-established scholars.[184]

Think tanks are in the business of shaping public opinion and public policy. Donald Abelson confirms that the Brookings Institution or the Council on Foreign Relations belong to the elite policy-planning organizations, but the vast majority of American think tanks - whose total number is roughly 2500 - has modest resources. Not all think tanks have the resources to advance an elite agenda, even though elite theorists see the political system as being dominated by the ruling class to promote its political, economic and social interests. "As appealing as the elite theory may be, it tells us little about the influence of think tanks at different stages of the policy cycle. It tells us even less about how to evaluate the impact of think tanks in policy-making. Unfortunately, the elite approach offers little insight how the right connections enable think tanks to influence public policy."[185]

Think tanks help define the boundaries of the policy debate, offer agendas and options, catalyse and popularise new ideas, help bridge the gaps between agencies and between the academic and policy worlds, provide advise to policy makers and serve to educate and inform Congress, the media, policymakers, and the general public. Wiarda, an ex-neocon, concludes from his perch at AEI, that think tanks are new among the most important actors in Washington D.C. with major interest groups, political parties, and lobbying organizsations.[186] For elite theorist like Joseph Peschek, Thomas Dye and William Domhoff think tanks not only regularly interact with policy elites, they help comprise part of the nation's power structure. Particularly in the US, think tanks serve in Donald Abelson's view as talent pools for incoming presidential administrations to draw on. Think tanks are portrayed as elite organizations well positioned to influence public policy because high-level policy-makers often take up residence at these research

[183] Wiarda, Howard: Conservative Brain Trust. The Rise, Fall, and Rise Again of the American Enterprise Institute. Lanham, Lexington Books, 2009 p. 4.
[184] McGann, James G.: The Competition for Dollars, Scholars and Influence in the Public Policy Research Industry . Lanham, University Press of America, 1995, p.27.
[185] Abelson, Donald E.: Do Think Tanks Matter? Assessing the Impact of Public Policy Institutes. 2nd Edition. Montreal, McGill-Quenn's University Press 2009, pp. 50-52.
[186] Wiarda, Howard: Conservative Brain Trust. The Rise, Fall, and Rise Again of the American Enterprise Institute. Lanham, Lexington Books, 2009 p. 62.

institutes after leaving office.[187] "Institutional procedures entail that the system responds better to the well-organised wealthy, skilled and knowledgeable than to disorganised, poorly financed, unskilled pressure groups."[188] According to elite theory, these networks are dominated by a small number of key actors, while Marxists claim that networks are dominated by interests representing capital. Though not Marxists, Peschek, Dye, Domhoff, Delgado or Krugman help explain how class power is translated into political rule, through the mediating role of corporate liberal policy-planning organizations. Following Antonio Gramsci, many Marxists see class rule as a complex process in which economic, political, cultural, and juridical actors and institutions are integrated into a hegemonic bloc. Intellectuals and professionals help establish and maintain the ideology of the ruling class by representing its ideas as in the general interest of society. But hegemony is never absolute in the Gramscian notion. Opposition to class rule is always present, along with systemic failures that can never be fully controlled by the power elites.[189]

"The public philosophy of the AEI might be described as ruling class Gramscianism. Gramsci argued that class rule in modern capitalist societies rests not only on state coercion and the compulsion of economic relationships, but also on the hegemony of a system of values, beliefs, and morality supportive of the existing order."[190] The close ties that exist between corporate and philanthropic donors and several think tanks suggest that think tanks often serve as instruments of the ruling elite.[191]

Think tanks may write legislation, prepare speeches or testimony, and lay out the policy options for decision-makers that were once the function of government policymakers.[192] In exchange for large donations, think tanks are willing according to elite theory to use their policy expertise and connections with key policy-makers to advance the political agendas of their generous benefactors.[193] "Think-tank analysts and position papers may even be telling elected

---

[187] Abelson, Donald E.: Do Think Tanks Matter? Assessing the Impact of Public Policy Institutes. 2nd Edition. Montreal, McGill-Queen's University Press 2009, p 50.
[188] Smith, James A.: The Idea Broker: Think Tanks and the Rise of the New Policy Elite. New York, Free Press 1991, p.3.
[189] Peschek, Joseph G.: Policy-Planning Organisations. Elite Agendas and America's Rightward Turn. Philadelphia, Temple University Press 1987, pp. 14-15.
[190] Ibid, p. 229.
[191] Abelson, Donald E.: Do Think Tanks Matter? Assessing the Impact of Public Policy Institutes. 2nd Edition. Montreal, McGill-Queen's University Press 2009, pp. 50 – 52.
[192] Wiarda, Howard: Conservative Brain Trust. The Rise, Fall, and Rise Again of the American Enterprise Institute. Lanham, Lexington Books, 2009 p. 4.
[193] Abelson, Donald E.: Do Think Tanks Matter? Assessing the Impact of Public Policy Institutes. 2nd Edition. Montreal, McGill-Queen's University Press 2009, pp. 50 – 52.

representatives how to vote on various issues."[194] From the Republican Contract with America to Bill Clinton's welfare reform and George W. Bush's plan of social security reform, all ideas came from research institutes.[195]

Formerly elitist scholars pursued research in relative isolation, they have now become widely visible in the political arena. Many of them have left the ivory tower to play an active part in American politics. On domestic and foreign policy, they have marketed their ideas to shape public opinion and public policy in forums, conferences, lectures at universities, congressional testimonies, op-ed articles in major newspapers, TV interviews and essays in Foreign Affairs by CFR and Foreign Policy by the Carnegie Endowment.[196]

Elite theorists suppose that the ruling classes employ the research institutes to exercise power. Conservative forces attempt to control and mobilise public opinion in the United States thanks to neoconservative intellectuals. Their policy entrepreneurship allows to introduce a policy change and to dominate the political agenda though their media coverage. The community of think tanks thus represents an undemocratic counter weight to the electorate. Though the political thinking of American voters is unified in conformity, think tanks remain in financial dependence from government and industry.[197] Political advocacy, a certain constituency or a political party demand a partisan research for scientific validation of an ideological world view. Among their staff, think tanks put higher value on ideological coherence than on academic qualifications.[198] Their studies are seen in public as bound to corporate interests and conservative policy circles. As a result, the Americans nourish anti-intellectualism and are discontent with their polarised society.[199]

---

[194] Wiarda, Howard: Conservative Brain Trust. The Rise, Fall, and Rise Again of the American Enterprise Institute. Lanham, Lexington Books, 2009 p. 4.
[195] Goodman, John C. (Präsident): National Center for Policy Analysis. In: McGann, James G.: Think Tanks and Policy Advice in the United States: Academics, Advisors and Advocates. New York, Routledge 2007, pp. 117 – 124 (p. 120).
[196] Abelson, Donald E: Think Tanks in the United States. In: Stone, Diane/ Denham, Andrew/ Garnett, Mark (eds.): Think Tanks Across Nations. A Comparative Approach. Manchester, Manchester University Press 1998, pp. 107 – 126, (p. 119)
[197] Stone, Diane/ Denham, Andrew/ Garnett, Mark (Eds.): Think Tanks Across Nations. Manchester, Manchester University Press 1998.
[198] McGann, James G.: Think Tanks and Policy Advice in the United States: Academics, Advisors and Advocates. New York, Routledge 2007, S. 15f.
[199] Stone, Diane/ Denham, Andrew/ Garnett, Mark (Eds.): Think Tanks Across Nations. Manchester, Manchester University Press 1998.

Government Contractors – Frontrunners of the Military-Industrial Complex?

While the existence of powerful factions in American society is nothing new – James Madison wrote about them two centuries ago – what is new is the emergence of think tanks as a central force in the political process. The legislative and executive branches have turned to outside experts to help solve complex problems and to manage a growing bureaucracy.[200] During World War II, Brookings guided the war mobilisation effort, and in the post war years, it designed the Marshall Plan. It provided the inspirations for many of Johnson's Great Society Programs of the 1960s. Yet, it was one of the most ardent opponents of Roosevelt's New Deal. Nevertheless, during the Kennedy, Johnson and Carter years, Brookings alienated itself from the business community by its support for Johnson's Great Society, and its opposition to the Vietnam War. The business community's disillusionment with Brookings led to the foundation of AEI, CSIS and Heritage Foundation which challenged Brookings' position. Brookings tried to alter its political image by hiring more Republicans to gain donations and to secure corporate contributions. Brookings moved to the center but left a hole on the liberal left which no major think tank occupied.[201]

By 1948, government contractors like RAND - an acronym for research and development - emerged in the US largely in response to the many new challenges the American diplomats inherited as the US assumed her role as hegemonic power in the atomic age. Acknowledging the invaluable contributions that defense scientists had made during the war the Truman administration continued to fund private expertise. Particularly in defense policy, it was crucial for the government to rely on the best defense scientists in the country in the assumption that unlike the political class these were unlikely to be influenced by partisan interests.[202] Federal research contract organisations are usually dependent on Pentagon funding. These institutes such as Rand are according to Diane Stone

---

[200] Mcgann, James G.: The Competition for Dollars, Scholars and Influence in the Public Policy Research Industry . Lanham, University Press of America, 1995, pp. 39-42.
[201] Ibid. pp. 134-139.
[202] Abelson, Donald E.: Do Think Tanks Matter? Assessing the Impact of Public Policy Institutes. 2nd Edition. Montreal, McGill-Queen's University Press 2009, p. 28 -29.

engaged in technical and defence related work and often maintain a close link to the military-industrial complex. Studies of strategy, logistics and armaments are dictated from government.[203] The second generation of think tanks such as the American Enterprise Institute for Public Policy Research (1946) and the RAND Corporation (1948) owe their origin almost entirely to the United States' increased international commitments after World War II. The military-industrial complex established these institutes to help sustain the defense spending generated during the war years. These institutes focus on different dimensions of national security and how to maintain it. The defense scientists founded conservative think tanks in both the domestic and foreign policy arena. AEI and RAND originated to a more conservative political and philosophical segment of American society and are organised in direct response to the perceived liberal threat created by institutions such as the Carnegie Endowment and the Council on Foreign Relations.[204]

After World War II, American policy-makers hoped to meet the new foreign policy challenges as the United States assumed its role as a hegemonic power by consulting the expertise of defense scientists. Washington provided government contractors with generous funding in exchange for expertise. "As a result, the reliance on government contracts and their strong ties to political leaders and high-level officials may have created the perception rightly or wrongly, that their policy advise is slanted." [205] RAND Corporation and CSIS became key players in the political arena during the 1950s and 60s.

These institutes serve government agencies and private sponsors on a contractual basis by executing research. Contract researchers cannot claim to be entirely objective in their studies, because if their conclusions are too much at odds with a client's interests, future research may be awarded to their competitors. The emphasis, here, then is on contract success rather than by the kind of peer group evaluation from epistemic communities.[206] Contract research therefore turns into political consultancy for governments and business lobbies which

---

[203] Stone, Diane: Capturing the Political Imagination. Think Tanks and the Policy Process. London, Frank Cass 1996, p.14.
[204] McGann, James G.: The Competition for Dollars, Scholars and Influence in the Public Policy Research Industry . Lanham, University Press of America, 1995, pp. 48-49.
[205] Abelson, Donald E: Think Tanks in the United States. In: Stone, Diane/ Denham, Andrew/ Garnett, Mark (eds.): Think Tanks Across Nations. A Comparative Approach. Manchester, Manchester University Press 1998, pp. 107 – 126, (p 112 - 113).
[206] Ricci, David: The Transformation of American Politics. The New Washington and the Rise of Think Tanks. New Haven, Yale University Press, 1993, p. 20.

prefer to outsource expert studies rather than conduct them in-house.[207] Think tanks like RAND, a leading government contractor in the second period from 1947 -70 rely primarily on government departments and agencies to sustain operations with an annual budget exceeding $200 million, RAND is nowadays one of America's premier defense policy institutes.[208] From 1962 on, the Center for Strategic and Defense Studies (CSIS) has rivaled with RAND for the rank of the most respected defense and foreign policy think tank in the US. Though its budgets exceed $ 20 million CSIS is known as home to former ambassadors, secretaries of defense and national security advisers (Brzesinksi and Kissinger). Each year, the idea factory convenes ca. 700 – 800 meetings, seminars, and conferences with policy-makers and scholars.[209]

Why did a massive proliferation of think tanks take place after World War II? First, as a result of casting aside its isolationist shell to assume the global responsibilities of a hegemonic power after World War II, the US had to rely increasingly on policy experts for advise on how to conduct its foreign relations, leading to the creation of AEI, RAND and CSIS.[210] Second, the impact of the anti-war and civil-rights movements in awakening the public conscience to political and social turmoil at home and abroad reflected in the growth of neoconservative and liberal think tanks during this period to challenge the consensus in the foreign policy establishment over America's role in the world. As conservative academics were disillusioned with what they considered to be a growing liberal bias among the faculty of American universities, an increasing demand for autonomous research in institutions like the Heritage Foundation emerged.[211]

The booming think tank industry in the United States following World War II not only altered policy-making in changing the relationship between policy experts and policy-makers.[212] In a milieu, where think tanks aggressively marketed their ideas, their priorities began to change, their policy expertise be-

---

[207] Wallace, William: Conclusion. Ideas and Influence. In: Stone, Diane/ Denham, Andrew/ Garnett, Mark (Eds.): Think Tanks Across Nations. Manchester, Manchester University Press 1998, pp. 223-230, (p. 226).
[208] Abelson, Donald E.: Do Think Tanks Matter? Assessing the Impact of Public Policy Institutes. 2nd Edition. Montreal, McGill-Queen's University Press 2009, p. 9.
[209] Ibid, pp. 185 -186.
[210] Abelson, Donald E: Think Tanks in the United States. In: Stone, Diane/ Denham, Andrew/ Garnett, Mark (eds.): Think Tanks Across Nations. A Comparative Approach. Manchester, Manchester University Press 1998, pp. 107 – 126, (p. 115)
[211] Ehrman, John: The Rise of Neoconservatism. Intellectuals and Foreign Affairs 1945 – 1994. New Haven, Yale University Press 1995.
[212] Abelson, Donald E: Think Tanks in the United States. In: Stone, Diane/ Denham, Andrew/ Garnett, Mark (eds.): Think Tanks Across Nations. A Comparative Approach. Manchester, Manchester University Press 1998, pp. 107 – 126, (p. 118)

came increasingly politicised.[213] Elite theorists, like Peschek, Domhoff and Dye, examined the role of think tanks and tried to prove their political influence by the revolving door principle, by the participation of well-known politicians in their seminars and conferences, by their scholars' testimonies in congressional hearings, and their assistance in election campaigns.[214] In the political system of the USA parties loose their importance in an increasingly decentralised and fragmented political environment.[215] In this context the undue influence of the "military industrial complex" or "iron triangles" is called into question: a sworn-in network of scientists, journalists, managers, bureaucrats and former policymakers allegedly uses its connections to put pressure on current decision-makers for realising its elitist agenda and securing financial interests.[216]

In times of crisis Americans look to the President the commander-in-chief, but not to Congress even though the US constitution gives the legislative great powers in US foreign policy. While the Congress was empowered in the control of presidential emergency rights in the Watergate scandal in the 1970s, nowadays Congress shows no interest to confront the President.[217] And in times of crisis presidents turn to their advisers before, contrary to state theory[218], they make difficult choices.[219] The Bush doctrine combines military strategy with the promotion of democracy. The United States conceives herself as protector of the defenders of liberty, peace and human dignity in the war against tyrants and terrorists. Traditionally, the USA serves, in Colin Powell's view, as light and ideal for the global expansion of liberalism.[220] American values are universal values whose global diffusion and acceptance stand for the national interest of the USA

---

[213] Ibid, p 124.

[214] Reinicke, Wolfgang H.: Lotsendienste für die Politik: Think Tanks – amerikanische Erfahrungen und Perspektiven für Deutschland. Gütersloh 1996, S. 39 und 46f.

[215] Braml, Josef: Deutsche und amerikanische Think Tanks. Voraussetzungen für ihr Wirken. Wissenschaft und Frieden 2004 – 4: Think Tanks. In www.wissenschaft-und-frieden.de/seite.php?artikelId=0337, pp. 1-5 (p. 5). [July 31st, 2009]

[216] Hennis, Michael: Der neue Militärisch-Industrielle Komplex in den USA. APuZ, B46/2003, S. 41-46.

[217] Sheffer, Martin S.: Presidential War Powers and the War on Terrorism: Are We Destined to Repeat Our Mistakes? In: Davis, John: The Global War on Terrorism: Assessing the American Response. New York 2004, pp. 27-44 (p. 28).

[218] "The state does act independently of various societal and bureaucratic pressures. Rather than allowing special interest groups to impose their agendas on the state, the president and his senior ministers ultimately determine the fate of the nation". Abelson, Donald E.: A Capitol Idea. Think Tanks and U.S. Foreign Policy. Montreal 2006, p. 98.

[219] Ibd., S. 120.

[220] Powell, Colin: A Strategy of Partnerships. In: Foreign Affairs, 2004, Jg. 83, Nr. 1, pp 22- 34. (p 34).

according to Condoleeza Rice. US foreign policy must assign highest priority to her national interest: the military superiority in power politics.[221]

American political scientists criticise the neoconservative militarisation of American society, the increasing executive power in relation to Congress and the displacement of the State Department by the Pentagon. Endorsing the theory of hegemonic stability that favours a world economy under US primacy neocons strongly back the assumption that the international system cannot afford a multipolar balance of power politics because of inevitable dangers and chaos.[222]

The economic and social policies of neocons resemble neoliberal plans of tax cuts for the wealthy that are financed by drastic cuts in the health care system and the welfare state resulting in the privatisation of Medicare and Medicaid and turning according to the Democrats the New Deal obsolete. In addition, critics attribute the astronomic foreign debts of the USA to the imperial overstretch generating from the ambitious military agenda.[223] National security thus serves as public legitimacy of a massive federal debt burden that forever prevents the extension of the welfare state.[224] German political scientists accuse the USA of unilaterally pursuing her national interests without concern for international law, international obligations or institutions. Multilateralism justifies and legitimises US foreign policy and reduces costs. In globally securing US hegemony, war is seen in Clausewitz terms as the continuation of politics by other means; in other words, war serves as a legitimate instrument of US foreign policy.[225]

---

[221] Rice, Condoleeza: Promoting the National Interest. In: Foreign Affairs, 2000, Jg. 79, Nr. 1, pp. 45-62. (p. 47-48.).

[222] Jervis, Robert: American Foreign Policy in a New Era. New York 2005. S. 90.

[223] Wilson, Hall T.: Capitalism After Postmodernism. Neo-conservatism, Legitimacy and the Theory of Public Capital. Leiden 2002, pp. 63-67.

[224] Hennis, Michael: Der neue Militärisch-Industrielle Komplex in den USA. APuZ, B46/2003, pp. 41-46 (p. 46).

[225] Rudolf, Peter: USA - Sicherheitspolitische Konzeptionen und Kontroversen. In: Ferdowsi, Mir A. (ed.): Sicherheit und Frieden zu Beginn des 21. Jahrhunderts. München 2002, pp. 149- S.163 (p. 160-161).

Foundations, Corporate Philanthropy and Political Advocacy

Scholars from think tanks have considerable influence in all spheres of American society. In David Ricci's opinion, increasing knowledge promised social security which led to the founding of think tanks in the Progressive Era. This optimistic belief in progress reflected the consultation of such an elite group of wise men. The US administration made the assumption that scholarly advise would serve the public interest rather than self-interest. Indeed, the political leadership in Washington was convinced of the Platonic notion of a voluntary academic who fulfils his public duty to the amateur under compliance of ethical standards for the benefit of his client. Of course, the observer should not take at face value the honorary intention of the human mind; Aristotle, himself, had for this reason rejected the Platonic rule of the philosopher-kings.[226]

Policy research institutes are distinguishable from philanthropic foundations which tend to fund research rather than to do it themselves. Institutions such as the Carnegie Endowment and Russell Sage Foundation are different from foundations that make grants as they use their own funds to conduct policy analysis and research. In contrast to consultancies, advocacy groups, interest groups and lobbies the research agenda is determined by the think tanks' board of directors, rarely by outside interests. Compared to interest groups that are more interested in grass-roots activity and advocacy, Diane Stone concludes that the policy research institute is founded for research not for profit.[227]

A component of American exceptionalism is the peculiarly robust private philanthropic sector which has traditionally existed in the USA. As Carol Weiss has pointed out, in no other country have the resources on which all think tanks ultimately depend been so richly available. The American political system provides think tanks with uniquely favourable opportunities not only to emerge, but also to gain access to decision-makers and so exert political influence. Con-

---

[226] Ricci, David M: The Transformation of American Politics. The New Washington and the Rise of Think Tanks. New Haven, Yale University Press, 1993, p. 15.
[227] Stone, Diane: Capturing the Political Imagination. Think Tanks and the Policy Process. London, Frank Cass 1996, p.13.

versely, America think tanks may find it more difficult than it is sometimes assumed to have an impact because the US political system is so competitive. As
Weiss notes the number of players in the policy game in Washington is legion.
Hence, American think tanks have to compete not only among themselves, but
also with a huge number of other lobbyists in order to persuade policy-makers in
both the executive and legislative branches of government to adopt a particular
policy or more ambitiously still embrace an entire agenda for policy.[228]Although
Stone admits that many think tanks conduct research in a simplified form. On the
one hand, policy institutes fade into interest groups which are increasingly recognising the value of research and analysis in policy debate. On the other hand,
think tanks merge with university bodies. Whereas from another angle, they
seem to become extra-political campaigning groups. Transition tanks have
emerged to provide advise for new incoming presidents. Presidential hopefuls set
up their own think tank to develop policy agendas but into which they can channel campaign contributions. The non-profit status of the think tank allows the
candidate to avoid compliance with federal limits on campaign contributions.[229]

The growth of third wave conservative advocacy institutions, in particular, was largely driven by generous benefactors who believed that with sufficient
funding think tanks could have a significant impact in shaping the political dialogue.[230] The steady rise in the political influence of the New Right, hard-line
anticommunists, free-market advocates and neoconservatives was made possible
by the funding of the business community (Coors, Chase Manhattan Bank, Hew-
lett-Packard, Texas Instruments) as well as by donations from right-wing foundations (Olin, Scaife, Smith-Richardson).[231]

Peschek blames the small chances of upward social mobility for wor-
king-class children in elitist think tanks. Most experts are recruited from the upper middle class. The majority of its directors are selected from the male white
Anglo-Saxon upper class.[232] Although many donors may pursue the amelioration
of societal sorrows for all Americans as reason for their philanthropy, one cannot
deny that rich patrons want to implement their own agenda: Carnegie, Ford, Mac
Arthur, Rockefeller, Buffett, Gates, Hewlett, Packard, Scaife, and Soros. Casting

---

[228] Weiss, Carol: Introduction: Helping Government Think: Functions and Consequences of Policy
Analysis Organisations. In: Weiss, Carol (Ed.) Organisations for Policy Advice. Helping Government
Think. London, Sage 1992, pp. 6-8.
[229] Stone, Diane: Capturing the Political Imagination. Think Tanks and the Policy Process. London,
Frank Cass 1996, pp. 12-17.
[230] Abelson, Donald E.: Do Think Tanks Matter? Assessing the Impact of Public Policy Institutes.
2nd Edition. Montreal, McGill-Queen's University Press 2009, p. 34
[231] Peschek, Joseph G.: Policy-Planning Organisations. Elite Agendas and America's Right-Ward
Turn. Philadelphia, Temple University Press 1987, pp. 27- 34.
[232] Ibid, p. 10.

a shadow on their independence, think tanks, however, need their donations because their income from publications and small donors is not enough to finance their activities. The financial rivalry leads to specialisation in issues, in agenda formulation and ideology.[233] The multimillion-dollar budgets of some US think tanks and prominent corporate leaders and former politicians on their boards of directors illustrate think tanks as policy elites. Large corporations and philanthropic foundations turn to like-minded think tanks in order to influence public policy. For preserving large budgets, think tanks try to mould public policy to their donors' benefit. In an increasingly competitive marketplace of ideas research institutes are more ready to give up their neutrality and credibility.[234]

While think tanks are engaged in scholarly research and activities they do not resemble universities. They are not involved in teaching and do not have the same disciplines. Research fellows at the universities without students are employees and not free to follow their intellectual priorities without constraint but are required to pursue organisational objectives. But academic freedom is not openly limited. Policy relevance is emphasised over academic research though researchers generally can draw their own conclusions. "While many of these institutes undertake extensive analysis, it is intended primarily to advance the cause of the association and to give them ammunition to use in the policy wars".[235]

According to Rich, experts are political actors and think tanks are among the most active and efficient political institutions. In practice, think tanks all too often diminish their influence by devoting resources and efforts on commentary to current legislature. Think tank commentary most often serves as ammunition for policymakers. Media visibility and permanent presence in the news represents a return on their investments for their donors. "The media attention validates the investments patrons make in a think tank's work. Furthermore policymakers need public justification for their already preferred policy choices".[236]

> "The proliferation of private foundations, the ease with which charitable donations for public purposes can be set against tax provide a firm financial base for intellectual diversity. Availability of public funding from competing agencies with government and Congress widens opportunities further. The separation of powers and the openness of policy negotiation within Washington gives easy access to those who wish to influence the debate,

---

[233] McGann, James G.: Think Tanks and Policy Advice in the United States: Academics, Advisors and Advocates. New York, Routledge 2007, pp. 45-47.
[234] Abelson, Donald E.: Do Think Tanks Matter? Assessing the Impact of Public Policy Institutes. 2nd Edition. Montreal, McGill-Queen's University Press 2009, p 50 -52.
[235] Stone, Diane: Capturing the Political Imagination. Think Tanks and the Policy Process. London, Frank Cass 1996, p.13.
[236] Rich, Andrew: Think Tanks, Public Policy, and the Poltics of Expertise. Cambridge, Cambridge University Press 2004, pp. 210-213.

while encouraging policy protagonists to look around for supporting arguments to help press their case. No other political system offers such an open and dispersed policy debate which think tanks can operate, not such diverse and generous sources of public and private finance."[237]

Writing a thesis on the war of ideas in American politics requires the examination of the role of foundations, universities, and advocacy and research organisations in efforts to shape the terms of debate in policy-making.[238] Generous corporate financing and tax exemptions for non-profit organisations provided an incentive for policy entrepreneurs, political leaders and office holders to create think tanks. By establishing private think tanks as non-profit organisations, corporations and philanthropic foundations contributed millions of dollars of support, to advance their particular ideological views on domestic and foreign policies. [239] This work diminishes their influence with policy makers. Their aggressive ideological marketing damages the reputation of experts among politicians. Experts produce in the words of Andrew Rich research that is little more than "polemical commentary".[240] The war of ideas taking place in newspapers and on TV illustrates the permanent presence of think tank scholars in US media and at universities.[241]

Many contemporary think tanks have undertaken enormous efforts and invested all their resources in ideologically influencing the public opinion and the policymaking.[242] Particularly advocacy think tanks try to play an active role in the political arena. In other words, they pursue to dominate the public debate for influencing the electorate and the representatives in prominent policy issues.[243] Like corporations, these institutes apply the most effective marketing

---

[237] Wallace, William: Conclusion. Ideas and Influence. In: Stone, Diane/ Denham, Andrew/ Garnett, Mark (Eds.): Think Tanks Across Nations. Manchester, Manchester University Press 1998, pp. 223-230, (pp. 227-228).
[238] Abelson, Donald E. "The Business of Ideas: The Think Tank Industry in the United States," in Diane Stone and Andrew Denham (eds), Think Tank Traditions. Manchester: Manchester University Press, 2004, pp. 215-31.
[239] Abelson, Donald E. Think Tanks in the United States, in Diane Stone, Andrew Denham and Mark Garnett (eds), Think Tanks Across Nations: A Comparative Approach. Manchester: Manchester University Press, 1998: pp. 107-126 (p. 117)..
[240] Rich, Andrew: Think Tanks, Public, Policy, and the Politics of Expertise.Cambridge, Cambridge University Press 2004, pp. 214 -215.
[241] Abelson, Donald E. "From Policy Research to Political Advocacy: The Changing Role of Think Tanks in American Politics." The Canadian Review of American Studies 25 (1) Winter 1995: 93-126.
[242] Higgott, Richard/Stone, Diane: The Limits of Influence: Foreign Policy Think Tanks in Britain and the USA. Review of International Studies, Vol. 20, No.1 (Jan. 1994), pp. 15 –34 (p. 29). In. www.jstor.org/stable/ 20097355 [July 31st 2009].
[243] Haas, Richard. N.: Think Tanks and U.S. Foreign Policy. A Policy-Maker's Perspective. In: The Role of the Think Tanks in U.S Foreign Policy. U.S. Foreign Policy Agenda. An Electronic Journal

strategies for the promotion of their ideas. Thus, think tanks have lost a lot of their integrity on the market place of ideas.[244] Because of their close ties to top-ranking politicians and bureaucrats think tanks obtain millions from corporate and philanthropic donor who wish to implement their conservative agenda into policy.[245]

The politicisation of policy research was caused by the political advocacy of the Heritage Foundation established in 1973. In McGann's view, Heritage was less a think tank than first and foremost an ideology factory, a marketing agency for the neoconservative movement. Its goal of a conservative nation is at odds with Brookings' objective analysis of critical policy concerns. Politicisation of expertise emanated from right-wing foundations that donated to specific projects to further the conservative mission partly due to the increasing influence of the media on American government.[246]

"While AEI focuses on policy analysis more than on scholarly research, producing technical reports for government agencies, Heritage produces non-technical policy analysis and prepares digests and recommendations for policymakers. Brookings, on the contrary, employs an academic scientific approach to its research, that produces book-length studies marketed to policymakers and academics."[247] In contrast to consultancies, advocacy groups, interest groups and lobbies the research agenda is determined by the think tanks' board of directors, rarely by outside interests.[248] Nevertheless much of the behavior of those in Washington D.C. is characterised by partisanship and ideological divisiveness that generally carry over to the general environment for experts and expertise.[249]

The polarisation between liberals and conservatives, the short-term orientation of donors and politicians but also the expectation of sensationalistic headlines by journalists forced the think tanks to align. The political routine in the nation's capital is characterised by the war of ideas. The political confrontation has risen to a new high in American politics. Think tanks provide with their studies new ammunition in the battle of good versus evil that dominates the American lawmakers' thinking. Only with long-term financing and the compliance to high academic standards these research institutes can preserve their independence.

---

of the Department of State. Vol. 7, No. 3 (Nov. 2002), p. 5-8. In: www. scribd.com/doc/3210628/the-role-of-the-think-tank-in-us-foreign-policy [August 2nd 2009].

[244] Abelson, Donald E.: *A Capitol Idea. Think Tanks and U.S. Foreign Policy.* Montreal 2006, p. IX.

[245] Thunert, Martin: „Think Tanks in Deutschland – Berater der Politik?" APuZ B51/2003, pp. 30 – 38 (p. 34).

[246] McGann, *The Competition for Dollars*, pp. 51-53.

[247] Ibid., p. 54.

[248] Stone, *Capturing the Political Imagination*, p. 13.

[249] Rich, *Think Tanks*, pp. 214 -215.

Advocacy Tanks Acting like Policy Entrepreneurs?

The critic of government, in parliament, in business, in party hierarchy, pressure groups, think tanks and the media offices searches for informed criticism from a preferred alternative perspective. New issues crowd onto the public agenda on which generalist policy makers must turn to the competing recommendations of expert advisors before they can grasp the choices to be made. The political demand for the services which think tanks can offer is thus likely to increase further. It is quite possible that the supply of institutionalised expertise, packaged in different ways to fit the requirements of political debate and policy-makers will continue to grow in response to demand.[250]

Institutions such as AEI and Brookings, in the face of criticism from some of their supporters and from policymakers responded to the needs of the policymaking community. Both of these institutions now produce summaries of studies by their scholars and develop them into policy briefs for policymakers. There is a tension between influencing partisan public policy and serving academic standards and independent analysis. Advocacy think tanks, thus, are determined by the needs of the client. They have chosen to advance a particular cause, constituency or ideology. Because they exist to promote an agenda that fosters their client's cause they are in the business of marketing and selling ideas. Their goal is to influence policy with pithy policy briefs and recommendations. As policy entrepreneurs, their independence and the objectivity of their research is called into question.[251]

Striking a suitable balance between neutrality - careful study and recommendation - and advocacy - aggressive persuasion and agitation - is not a new challenge for think tanks.[252] Andrew Rich suggests that "think tanks more easily sustained a balance of influence and credibility through the 1960s because

---

[250] Wallace, William: Conclusion. Ideas and Influence. In: Stone, Diane/ Denham, Andrew/ Garnett, Mark (Eds.): Think Tanks Across Nations. Manchester, Manchester University Press 1998, pp. 223-230, (pp. 229 -230).

[251] McGann, James G.: The Competition for Dollars, Scholars and Influence in the Public Policy Research Industry . Lanham, University Press of America, 1995, pp. 72-74.

[252] Rich, Andrew: Think Tanks, Public Policy, and the Poltics of Expertise. Cambridge, Cambridge University Press 2004, p. 29.

the policymaking environment for think tanks valued objective expertise and because the funding environment for think tanks accommodated, even encouraged, their combined pursuit of credibility and low-profile influence with decision-makers. Beginning in the 1960s, American politics became more ideologically divisive. The number of politically committed and active conservatives grew substantially after Barry Goldwater's 1964 presidential campaign. The business community recommitted itself to engaging in the policymaking process. They also created more ideological conservative think tanks whose strategies consisted in aggressive marketing of research."[253]

Known for marketing and repacking ideas than for generating them, advocacy think tanks have played a critical role in transforming the complexion of the policy research community. Advocacy think tanks tend to place greater emphasis on producing brief reports for policy makers than on producing book-length studies. Moreover to influence public opinion and public policy, these institutes also placed a high premium on gaining access to the media. Their scholars have frequently appeared on political talk shows to promote their agenda.[254]

James McGann concluded from his "visit to the Heritage Foundation that it is much run like a newspaper; weekly editorial meetings are held to set production schedules, identify hot issues and develop marketing strategies and policy angles. The dominant culture is clearly a corporate/ journalistic one rather than the university/ academic culture that is so prevalent at other research institutes in and around the Beltway. Heritage thus applies what has become known as the brief-case test to all its products: they must be short and to the point so that they can be read by members of Congress in the time it takes to ride Washington National Airport to Capitol Hill."[255]

Weaver has described think tanks as policy entrepreneurs operating in a distinct political system characterised by the division of powers between the President and Congress, weak and relatively non-ideological parties and the permeability of administrative elites. Scholars at think tanks act as policy entrepreneurs, first, by promoting ideas and placing them on the public agenda and second by "softening-up" actors in the political system to opportunity windows.[256]

---

[253] Rich, Andrew: Think Tanks, Public Policy, and the Poltics of Expertise. Cambridge, Cambridge University Press 2004, pp. 30-31.
[254] Abelson, Donald E.: Do Think Tanks Matter? Assessing the Impact of Public Policy Institutes. 2nd Edition. Montreal, McGill-Queen's University Press 2009,p. 20
[255] McGann, James G.: The Competition for Dollars, Scholars and Influence in the Public Policy Research Industry . Lanham, University Press of America, 1995, pp. 130-131.
[256] Weaver, R. Kent: The Changing World Think Tanks. PS: Political Science and Politics. Sept. 1989, pp. 563 – 578 (p.570).

In the late 1960s the conservatives founded advocacy think tanks in the USA for containing the undue influence of liberal research institutes like the Brookings Institution. Advocacy Tanks are obviously linked to a political party. These policy entrepreneurs actively pursue to influence the political debate by implementing their ideas and proposals.[257] Their studies are typically papers rather than book-length monographs. Weaver argues what their publications may lack in scholarly credentials is substituted by their contacts to politicians.[258]

For Sidney Blumenthal, the emergence of conservative think tanks, in particular, is attributable to the efforts of conservative intellectuals along with corporate and ideological patrons who formed think tanks and other organisations in order to disrupt the political status quo.[259] David Ricci argues that the number of think tanks has grown and become more ideological since the 1960s to accomodate greater general uncertainty in the conduct of American politics from the 1960s onwards, and to meet a demand for active debate over policy ideas and directions. Ricci views think tanks as a logical outgrowth of a reorientation of American elites that feared ideas and ideologies of the role of government, the rise of minorities and confusion over national purposes in the political process.[260]

When it was formed in 1973 by Paul Weyrich and Edwin Feulner, The Heritage Foundation crafted strategies for informing lawmakers to improve those of the AEI. From its beginning, the Heritage Foundation made informing congressional decision-making central to its mission. The formation of Heritage marked a turning point for think tanks in influencing policy-makers' thinking through promotion of their research in the media. Experts more easily find access to policy-makers when they are viewed as credible by the general public. That is why expertise must be timely and marketed. Prominent experts become politically active thus the scholars become advocates, promoters and defenders.[261]

James Smith, however, attributes the success of ideological think tanks to both change in the environment and to the more active efforts of political elites. Smith describes how conservative intellectuals propagated an anti-statist philosophy that contributed to the ideological conflict in the 1970s. Conserva-

---

[257] Homolar-Riechmann: Pax Americana und die gewaltsame Demokratisierung. Zu den politischen Vorstellungen der neokonservativen Think Tanks. APuZ, B46/2003, pp. 33-40.
[258] Weaver, R. Kent: The Changing World Think Tanks. PS: Political Science and Politics. Sept. 1989, pp. 563 – 578 (p.567).
[259] Blumenthal, Sidney: The Rise of the Counter-Establishment. From Conservative Ideology to Political Power. New York, Times Books. 1986.
[260] Ricci, David M.: The Transformation of American Poltics. The New Washington and the Rise of Think Tanks. New Haven, Yale University Press 1993, p. 208.
[261] Rich, Andrew: Think Tanks, Public Policy, and the Poltics of Expertise. Cambridge, Cambridge University Press 2004, pp. 151-155

tives built an infrastructure of think tanks to expand political debates to change decision-making in American politics. Ideas were seen as the means to overturn the liberal establishment and replacing it by an establishment of their own, conservatives founded and strengthened hundreds of think tanks.[262] Ideological think tanks, according to Rich, pursue an interest in making their points of view known among policy-makers and the general public. Acting as agents of ideologies rather than as independent analysts they want to fight for a particular policy. Moreover, their funders want to see media visibility as an immediate sign of success. That is why think tanks may draw the attention of most policy makers and journalists when issues are under final deliberation. The attention the work received then serves as an indicator for political influence of think tanks.[263]

Corporations, individuals, and ideological foundations have barely interest in waiting years to see a return on investment. A pool of experts does not only evaluate policy but works for the administration. These scholars offer credible studies and solutions to public problems which they promote in media interviews and public forums.[264] Scholars are producing inexpensive, reliable, and highly marketable commentary. Their patronage does not finance long-term costly projects.[265]

Therefore, advocacy tanks have only emerged since the 1960s and combine a strong policy, partisan or ideological outlook with aggressive salestechniques. In a deliberate effort to influence the course of current policy debates advocacy tanks repackage existing research rather than conduct new enquiries Advocacy think tanks are frequently difficult to distinguish from pressure groups in that both are essentially interested in political lobbying.[266] According to Rich think tanks compete with NGOs involved in policy debates, especially interests groups and lobbyists that almost invariably have more resources and power than they do.[267] An important difference between the two, however in Weaver's view, is that think tanks tend to cooperate across a broad range of policy areas, whereas the pressure groups organise their activities on particular issues.[268]

---

[262] Smith, James A.: The Idea Brokers. New York, Free Press 1991, p. 182.

[263] Rich, Andrew: Think Tanks, Public Policy, and the Poltics of Expertise. Cambridge, Cambridge University Press 2004, pp. 210 – 213.

[264] Homolar-Riechmann, Alexandra: Pax Americana und die gewaltsame Demokratisierung. Zu den politischen Vorstellun-gen der neokonservativen Think Tanks. APuZ, B46/2003, S. 33-40.

[265] Rich, Andrew: Think Tanks, Public Policy, and the Poltics of Expertise. Cambridge, Cambridge University Press 2004, pp. 210 – 213.

[266] Weaver, R. Kent: The Changing World Think Tanks. PS: Political Science and Politics. Sept. 1989, pp. 563 – 578 (p.567).

[267] Rich, Andrew: Think Tanks, Public Policy, and the Poltics of Expertise. Cambridge, Cambridge University Press 2004, pp. 214 – 215.

[268] Weaver, R. Kent: The Changing World Think Tanks. PS: Political Science and Politics. Sept. 1989, pp. 563 – 578 (p.567).

Whereas Rich recognises the difficulty that think tanks and experts generally become politically active at the moment when the media demands scholarly opinion, then the nature of their activity undermines their influence.[269] Experts can have a meaningful impact on how new problems are defined. Proposals that reach interested policy makers as they prepare action on an issue can provide substantive help to them. Policy makers ultimately seek to manipulate the story to suit their political goals. But experts offer early guidance on the dimensions of new problems, often laying the substantive foundations for how new issues evolve in public opinion. In some instances, proposals can convince policy makers to take action. The researcher may provide justification for the views of policy makers. The Heritage Foundation's efforts to build support for a Missile Defense is an example.[270]

While many of these groups undertake extensive analysis, it is intended primarily to advance the cause of the association and to give them ammunition to use in the policy wars. Interest groups are more interested in grass-roots activity and advocacy whereas the policy research institute is first and foremost a research outfit not profit.[271] "Experts act as advocates, whereas advocates pass as experts." [272] By responding to politics, ideology and marketing oppressed credibility and independence. Some think tanks therefore ignored academic standards. Think tanks market polemical commentary rather than pursuing neutral research.

Neoconservatives are blamed for acting like policy engineers whose intellectual fallacy for ideological policies is deduced from the corporate patronage for their studies. Their donors buy with cash the researchers' credibility to indirectly influence policy-making. Often advocacy tanks propose one standard solution to complex problems: limited government. The policy advocates make profits from their expertise. Their networks with managers, politicians and journalists initiate the politicisation of knowledge. Their research findings have a partisan character and pursue the sole aim of defeating the liberals in the war of ideas. Scholars are prone to political pressure and are tempted by material interests.[273] Although their expertise should serve the nation. Foreign policy is about comprehending major contextual and environmental changes taking place in the world and think tank scholars should steer, direct, and influence the impact of those trends over a reasonable time frame.

---

[269] Rich, Think Tanks,, pp. 214 – 215.
[270] Ibid, pp. 214 – 215.
[271] Stone, Capturing the Political Imagination, p. 13.
[272] Rich, Think Tanks, ,pp. 214 -215.
[273] Stone, Diane/ Denham, Andrew/ Garnett, Mark (eds.): Think Tanks Across Nations. Manchester, Manchester University Press 1998.

The Role of Neoconservative Think Tanks in US Foreign Policy

The Heritage Foundation and the American Enterprise Institute became under Reagan and Bush jr. the ideological headquarters of the Republican Party which led to a direct involvement in both conservative administrations and as critics claim to a promotion of elitist ambitions of their donors from industry and commerce. In this sense, neoconservatives are accused to act like policy engineers because of the patronage from business sectors and to foster an intellectual predisposition for ideological policies. Their donors ante up money to back mediately their political demands with studies and the academic reputation of the scholars towards the government. The polarisation of American Politics can thus be ascribed to the research institutes namely to the phenomenon of the "revolving door": from ambitious carreerists who move from the think-tank industry or from universities into government jobs in the USA.[274]

Think tanks, according to the elite theory, utilise their contacts for advancing the political and economic interests of their donors – the ruling class.[275] In this context, the military-industrial complex is often mentionned in the US: a network of scholars, managers and former politicians who influence officeholders for guarding their elitist and financial interests; a political lobbyism which is officially prohibited but allows former high-ranking state employees to write their memoirs.[276] With good reason the citizen increasingly asks who rules the country.

James Madison, one of the authors of the Federalist Papers, wanted the separation of powers to stop lobbies without a mandate from obtaining control over national policies.[277] Doubts arise regarding the network of policymakers, journalists, business leaders and researchers if these misuse their political influence and

---

[274] Stone, Diane/ Garnett, Mark: "Introduction: Think Tanks, Policy Advice and Governance". Diane Stone, Andrew Denham and Mark Garnett (Eds.): Think Tanks Across Nations. Manchester. Manchester University Press 1998, pp. 1-20.
[275] Abelson, Donald E.: A Capitol Idea. Think Tanks and U.S. Foreign Policy. Montreal, McGill-Queen's University Press 2006, pp. 97-99.
[276] Hennis, Michael: „Der neue Militärisch-Industrielle Komplex in den USA". Aus Politik und Zeitgeschichte, B46/(2003), 41-46.
[277] Abelson, Capitol Idea, 110.

their academic credibility to further the special interests of their patrons at cost of the common weal. Politicians and policy advisors are intimately connected in a network considering the ubiquitous presence in newspaper articles and interviews of think-tank scholars in the American media due to the war of ideas.[278] Because of weak party identification in the USA, a political system that encourages lawmakers to rather follow the wish of their voters and of organized interests than to toe to the party line, Congressmen need not fear that their proximity to a particular think tank and its ideas can undermine party unity.[279]

In the late 1960s, Conservatives founded advocacy think tanks in the US with the aim of containing the ominous influence of liberal research institutes like the Brookings Institution. Advocacy tanks are obviously aligned with a political party and actively try to affect the political debate with their ideas and policy proposals. A pool of experts does not only evaluate the current policies but also works for the administration.[280] Although their studies were misused for political means the scholars were considered until the 1970s as neutral and independent from the political establishment.[281] In reality, both the Heritage Foundation and the AEI have combined political advocacy with ideological research. Since the 1970s these advocacy tanks have given a higher priority to marketing and recycling of ideas than developing new concepts. In the past years it became according to Abelson increasingly difficult to discern between think tanks and interest groups.[282]

So advocacy think tanks are in conflict with scientific research standards and lose their credibility through a political agenda. Nevertheless they can find the financial support of kindred-spirits which can distort both their research program and their mission. Advocating a cause, a particular electorate or a party demands partisan scholarship for the scientific backup of a worldview. Within their staff the ideological closeness matters more than academic qualification.[283]

---

[278] McGann, James G.: "Academics to Ideologues: A Brief History of the Public Policy Research Industry". Political Science and Politics. Vol. 25. No.4 (Dec. 1992), pp. 733- 740. www.jstor.org/stable/419684 [Accessed Jan 31 2013].

[279] Higgott, Richard/ Stone, Diane: "The Limits of Influence: Foreign Policy Think Tanks in Britain and the USA". Review of International Studies, Vol. 20, No.1 (Jan. 1994),pp. 15 –34. www.jstor.org/stable/20097355 [Accessed Jan 31 2013].

[280] Alexandra Homolar-Riechmann: „Pax Americana und die gewaltsame Demokratisierung. Zu den politischen Vorstellungen der neokonservativen Think Tanks". Aus Politik und Zeitgeschichte, B46 (2003),pp. 33-40.

[281] Rochefort, David A./ Cobb, Roger W.: The Politics of Problem Definition. Shaping the Policy Agenda. Lawrence, University Press of Kansas 1994.

[282] Abelson, Do Think Tanks Matter? pp. 10-11.

[283] Abelson, Donald E.: American Think-Tanks and their Role in US Foreign Policy. London, MacMillan Press Ltd. 1996, p. 65.

Over the years right-wing foundations like Lynde, Bradley, Carthage and Koch have not only financed think tanks but also the education of conservative students to journalists, lobbyists, policy advisors, economists and lawyers. As loyal supporters of free-market economics this vanguard should promote the conservative agenda over the Republican Party to Capitol Hill and to the White House. This right-wing intelligentsia worked for a conservative media apparatus (namely FOX and Murdoch), in think tanks and interest groups to bring about a conservative turn in American Politics. In the 1970s a group of conservatives attempted with the financial support of right-wing foundations to create a nation-wide network from institutes and individuals to counter the liberal establishment and to shape federal policies in accordance with conservative ideas.[284]

The GOP was reinforced in the 1970s by the neoconservatives. These had turned away from the Democrats because of their liberal views on domestic politics and foreign policy. The neocons were attracted to conservative policies. Intellectuals like Irving Kristol, Jeane Kirkpatrick, Ben Wattenberg and Michael Novak were employed by well-funded conservative think tanks, mainly the American Enterprise Institute. There they proclaimed their doctrines of strong national defense and militant anti-communism alongside the economic strategy of deregulation and limited government.[285]

The accession to power of the right-wing in the GOP took place in the mid-1970s when the institutions of the conservative movement - think tanks such as the Heritage Foundation and the American Enterprise Institute – carried the political change to polarisation and unleashed the increasing economic inequality under Reagan.[286] The "war of ideas" was declared by the neocons at the AEI and the Heritage Foundation whereby they endeavoured laissez-faire in the free market.[287] Neocons in media, research institutes and the Republican Party were financed by philanthrophists and corporations to end the high tax burden on the wealthy by abolishing the welfare state and reversing the New Deal.[288]

---

[284] Ricci, David M.: The Transformation of American Politics. The New Washington and the Rise of Think Tanks. New Haven, Yale University Press, 1993, pp. 154 – 166. Kuttner, Robert: "Philanthrophy and Movements". The American Prospect July 15 2002. www. prospect.org/cs/articles?article=philanthropy_ and_movements. Covington, Sally: "How Conservative Philanthrophies and Think Tanks Transform US Policy". Covert Action Quarterly 1998. www.thirdworldtraveler/Democracy/ ConservThinkTanks.html.
[285] Easton, Nina J.: Gang of Five: Leaders at the Center of the Conservative Ascendancy. New York: Simon & Schuster 2000, pp. 23-47.
[286] Blumenthal, Sidney: The Rise of the Counter-Establishment: From Conservative Ideology to Political Power. New York: Time Books, 1986,pp. 38-39.
[287] Ricci, Transformation of American Politics, pp. 154 - 166.
[288] Peschek, Joseph G.: Policy-Planning Organizations: Elite Agendas and America's Rightward Turn. Philadelphia: Temple University Press 1987, p. 28.

The neoconservative think-tank scholars have constantly participated in conferences and briefings that were often broadcast on TV. In doing so, they discussed political issues with politicians, journalists and businessmen; this turned the academics in "public intellectuals". For expanding their influence on the power brokers the neocons had to capture and maintain the support of the research institutes. Since conservative think tanks employ mostly scholars with identical ideological views. Therefore, these institutes eased neoconservatism the perception as a distinct political movement and promoted their image as public intellectuals. The AEI contributed to the acceptance of neoconservative ideas and reinforced the connection between the neoconservative intellectuals and the political elites.[289] The stress on defense spending was mostly responsible to mobilise the business sector and particularly the arms manufacturers. Velasco accredits the rekindling of anti-communism and of American militarism to the new political strategy of the defense sector to pour money into conservative idea factories.[290]

Major corporations and the arms industry donated large sums to these institutes in hopes of influencing the policymakers. Rich companies and foundations promoted neoconservative journals, institutions and fellowships which enhanced neoconservative presence in the political arena in the US.[291] Businessmen like Joseph Coors, John M. Olin, Richard Mellon Scaife, Harry Bradley and the Koch brothers financed Heritage and AEI because they were worried with the swing to the left. They decided to fund a conservative "counterestablishment" for drawing America to the right.[292] In think tanks the neoconservatives founded journals to disseminate their ideas among the educated class. Furthermore, they created an institutional basis that emphasised their role as "public intellectuals". In the 1970s neoconservatives worked at the Center for Strategic and International Studies, the Hoover Institution, the Heritage Foundation and the AEI, the focal point of the neoconservative movement. From the beginning the neoconservatives have actively been involved in research institutes which has great importance in their relations to the power centre in Washington D.C.[293]

The old right complained bitterly that the neoconservatives had edged them out from think tanks and that they had exclusively won the financial aid of the foundations. Many of the traditional conservatives named themselves paleocon-

---

[289] Velasco, Jesús: Neoconservatives in U.S. Foreign Policy under Ronald Reagan and George W. Bush. Voices Behind the Throne. Washington D.C., Woodrow Wilson Center Press 2010, pp. 52-54.
[290] Ibid., p. 145.
[291] ibid., p. 168.
[292] Micklethwait, John/ Wooldridge, Adrian: The Right Nation. Conservative Power in America. New York, Penguin Books 2004, ´pp. 77-79.
[293] Velasco, Neoconservatives, p. 33.

servatives for differing from the neocons whose commitment to the conservative cause they suspected. In their view, these were opportunistic, devious, avid for power, ideological and not very religious. They were former Trotskiyists who pretended to having invented conservatism. Nonetheless, the greatest concern of the paleoconservatives remained the loss of their basis in AEI, the Hoover Institution, the Scaife, the Bradley, the Smith Richardson and the John M. Olin foundations.[294]

Neoconservatism might not be welcomed by some rightist circles but it provided the conservative movement energy and expertise in the 1980s. Neoconservatives believed that the GOP's rise to power depended on its ideologisation. The emergence of neoconservative policy advisers and the institutionalisation of conservatism in think tanks directly dared the liberal establishment.[295] When the neocons uttered their discontent think tanks appeared on the political stage for providing the Republican Party with much-needed expertise. Policy entrepreneurs such as William Baroody, Edwin Feulner and Paul Weyrich started to entrench conservatism in institutions. Their aim was to rival the liberal regime for the control of the sources of power. The appearance of think tanks changed the history of conservatism and left an enormous imprint on the Republican right in subsequent years.[296]

Thereof, neocons could propagate their opinion on foreign policy with unconstrained financial means. Their organisations upvalued the formation of the prominent political and intellectual movement because they strengthened the impact of neoconservatism in American foreign policy. Think tanks advanced the spreading of neoconservative ideas, coordinated the policy network, operated as centers of political organisation, provided advise to the political and economic elites and formed strongholds of intellectual deliberation. Think tanks constituted the structure for political intercourse between the neoconservatives and the power-holders in politics, business and media which facilitated both the access to the political agenda and to public opinion. In addition, the weakening of the political parties offered the research institutes room for manoeuver. With the media, the "public intellectuals" took over the task of educators of the American people.[297]

---

[294] Dorrien, Gary : Economy, Difference, Empire. Social Ethics for Social Injustice. New York, Columbia University Press 2010, p. 207.
[295] Crichtlow, Donald T.: The Conservative Ascendancy. How the Republican Right Rose to Power in Modern America. 2. edn. Lawrence, University Press of Kansas 2011, p. 122.
[296] Ibid.
[297] Arin, Kubilay Yado: Die Rolle der Think Tanks in der US Außenpolitik. Von Clinton zu Bush Jr. Wiesbaden, VS Springer 2013.

When Ronald Reagan came into office he selected several neoconservatives for service in his administration: Richard Perle, Jeane Kirkpatrick and Elliot Abrams became high-ranking members of the State Department and Pentagon. Though some of them like Kirkpatrick and Abrams were Democrats they nevertheless designed Reagan's foreign policy. Unlike these few neoconservatives remained Democrats which resulted in a coherent and strong foreign policy under their direction. Since the late 1980s and the early 1990s neoconservatism officially got an integral part of the Republican Party.

Under Reagan 32 members of the Committee on the Present Danger (CPD) were appointed to the State Department and the Pentagon. They had the ability to enforce strong anti-communism and the increase of military expenditure. In opposition to the liberal Council on Foreign Relations military officers, intelligence officials, neoconservative intellectuals and arms manufacturers were organised in the CPD. They regarded the riots in the Third World as a consequence of Soviet expansionism that challenged US hegemony. Therefore, these hardliners demanded a strong military build-up in conventional and nuclear weapons to counter this threat.[298]

The neocons also had reservations on Carter's foreign policy; because of their concern about the Soviet-Arab threat to Israel's existence they supported Reagan.[299] "Low intensity conflict" and unconventional CIA-promoted anti-communist uprisings should according to the Reagan Doctrine conceived by the Heritage Foundation cope with radical regimes in the Third World.[300] In the Cold War, the neoconservatives were strictly opposed to détente towards the Soviet Union and already advocated in those days US primacy. „The reason why the neoconservatives proved so influential was not because they deceived their fellow conservatives but because they succeeded in translating some of America's deepest passions into a theory of foreign policy." [301]

In the mid-1990s the neocons ensured their advance in the conservative movement, in the GOP and in Congress with money from Rupert Murdoch. Accordingly the "National Review" came under their influence.[302] The Weekly Standard, belonging to Murdoch, Commentary and The National Interest may not have high circulation but their articles are distributed through Murdoch's New York Post, his Wall Street Journal and Reverend Moon's Washington

---

[298] Peschek Policy-Planning Organizations, pp. 16-17.
[299] Wiarda, Howard: Conservative Brain Trust. The Rise, Fall, and Rise Again of the American Enterprise Institute. Lanham: Lexington Books 2009, 10.
[300] Peschek, Policy-Planning Organizations, pp. 160-62.
[301] Micklethwait and Wooldridge, Right Nation,p. 224.
[302] Ibid., p. 15.

Times to a broader audience.[303] The neoconservatives were heavily criticised for their aggressive foreign policy particularly in Somalia in the 1990s by the isolationists in the Republican Party. In addition, the unconditional neoconservative backing of Israel angered the isolationists around Pat Buchanan. Albeit the neoconservatives in opposition to the republican mainstream endorsed a liberal immigration policy.[304] The unifying factor of the communist threat had ceased. Nevertheless, neocons touted for a "unipolar" foreign policy that should found primacy over the entire world; the old right mistrusted their strategy. These accused the neocons to place a greater value to Israel whereat they charged their critics with anti-Semitism. Their rivals claimed that neoconservatives were driven by the national interest of Israel prior to the Iraq war neglecting America's security and economic interests.[305]

This chapter explores the change in US foreign policy in the Clinton and Bush jr. administrations from multilateralism to unilateralism under the influence of neoconservative think tanks. How can the transition from assertive multilateralism under Clinton to primacy under Bush jr. be explained? Is this alteration in foreign policy connected with the impact of neoconservative think tanks such as the American Enterprise Institute (AEI), the Heritage Foundation and the Project for a New American Century (PNAC) which manipulated as sectional interest groups the definition of expansive foreign policy goals at cost of broadly-conceived national interests?

After recruiting their staff from the most renowned think tanks the Clinton and Bush administrations succeeded in influencing the public opinion in the US. In this regard, policy advisers from think tanks are not merely viewed as objective scholars who give neutral recommendations to the government but as policy entrepreneurs who are associated with power blocs, foundations, corporations and partisan politics. I argue that these advocates of ideological change and political reorientation attempted to transform the political agenda under Clinton and to use the international crisis after 9/11 under Bush jr. in favour and in the interest of their donors from business, media and politics. Did the neoconservative PNAC form an alliance with the Bush Administration that left the US no other choice than to become the world's policeman?

In this chapter, the success of the neoconservative think tanks as advocacy coalition is discussed. For the conservative turn the alliance of the Christian Right and the neoconservative intellectuals in think tanks (Heritage Foundation and AEI) with the financial elite did not only move the Republican Party to the

---

[303] Ibid., pp. 10-11.
[304] Ibid., p. 15.
[305] Dorrien, Gary: Imperial Designs. Neoconservatism and the New Pax Americana. New York, Routledge 2004,pp. 196-98.

right but also tried to manipulate public opinion under the influence of sympa-
thising media tycoons like Rupert Murdoch.[306] Neoconservative papers like the
National Journal, the Public Interest and the American Spectator influence the
op-eds of the Wall Street Journal and the Washington Times. Liberal think tanks
and their contacts in Congress should be expelled from the government apparatus
by losing their donors with the result that the neocons could gain access to the
state institutions and leave an imprint on the Clinton administration before the
next election.[307]

In the wake of the "Republican Revolution" conservative think tanks were
preferably invited to congressional testimonies and also received more media
coverage than their liberal counterparts.[308] During the Gingrich administration
neoconservative think tanks proved that they did not want to stand idly by at the
sidelines of the power centre and wait for the election of a like-minded government. They were not discouraged to participate in the decision-making process;
on the contrary the neocons generated a huge effort to shape the agenda in important issues on domestic and foreign policies. They essayed to enlarge their
political support in Congress and in the bureaucracy. In an open letter to President Clinton the neocons were even successful to arouse his interest for their
ambitious plan of reordering the Middle East. Until 1997, the neoconservative
Project for a New American Century had developed plans for the invasion in
Iraq.[309] In the following, I suggest that under Clinton the unilateral tendencies
had been achieved above all by the Republican Congress while under George W.
Bush a Republican administration came into office which had reservations
against international agreements and multilateralism in general.

---

[306] Müller, Harald: „Das transatlantische Risiko – Deutungen des amerikanisch-europäischen
Weltordnungskonflikts". Aus Politik und Zeitgeschichte B 3-4/ (2004),pp. 43-44.
[307] Krugman, Paul: Nach Bush. Das Ende der Neokonservativen und die Stunde der Demokraten.
Bonn, Bundeszentrale für politische Bildung 2008,pp. 182-84.
[308] From 1998 to 2008 Heritage had more often been mentioned in Congress than the liberal Brookings Institution. In the same period conservative experts from AEI, CSIS, Heritage, Cato and RAND
had more often been invited to testimonies than Brookings before the Republican-controlled Congress. Abelson, Donald E.: Do Think Tanks Matter? Assessing the Impact of Public Policy Institutes.
2. edn., Montreal, McGill-Queen's University Press 2009, pp. 174-76.
[309] Coffman, Tom: "The American Antecedent in Iraq". Majid Tehranian and Kevin P. Clements
(Eds.): America and the World. The Double Bind. (New Brunswick: Transactions 2005), pp. 3-11.

The Clinton Administration

Large parts of the American people expected the balancing of the federal budget than leading in foreign policy. Thus, Clinton had promised with his "assertive multilateralism" a global commitment of the USA towards a multilateral coope-ration for both lowering the costs of US leadership and preventing American losses in the army. Not "hard power", i.e. military power, but "soft power" had priority; according to CSIS-fellow Joseph S. Nye soft power was the ability to capture the international agenda by means of political and cultural leadership for shaping international institutions and norms. Military force should only be used when national interests were threatened; apart from that democratisation of the world and international cooperation in multilateral institutions were given pre-ference.[310]

Clinton's strategy of "assertive multilateralism" failed before the Re-publican electoral success in Congress in 1994 because of the resistance of the Democrats in Congress and the negative attitude in media and public.[311] Clinton was reproached with weak leadership because he could not assert himself against the European allies and the UN neither in Somalia nor in the Balkans. The rejec-tion and the mistrust to international organizations seemed to be deeply rooted in the GOP and with their neoconservative advisers in think tanks such as AEI, Heritage Foundation and the Hoover Institution.[312]

The contest for power between the Republican-controlled Congress and the Democrat Clinton was hold at the expense of the international obligations of the USA, notably those towards the United Nations.[313] Though his Secretary of State Madeleine Albright, a former think-tank scholar, had pursued "assertive

---

[310] Nye, Joseph S.: Soft Power. The Means to Success in World Politics. New York, Public Affairs, 2004.

[311] Sterling-Folker, Jennifer: "Between a Rock and a Hard Place. Assertive Multilateralism and Post-Cold-War U.S. Foreign Policy". James M. Scott, (Ed.): After the End. Making U.S. Foreign Policy in the Post-Cold-War World. Durham: Duke University Press 1998, pp. 277 – 304.

[312] Arin, Kubilay Yado: Die Rolle der Think Tanks in der US Außenpolitik. Von Clinton zu Bush Jr. Wiesbaden, VS Springer 2013.

[313] Luck, : Edward C. "American Exceptionalism and International Organisation: Lessons from the 1990s". Rosemary Foot, / S. Neil MacFarlane and Michael Mastanduno (Eds.): US Hegemony and International Organizations. The United States and Multilateral Institutions. (Oxford: Oxford Univer-sity Press 2003),pp. 25-48.

multilateralism" in diplomacy, the president gave in to pressure from the Republican Congress and their neoconservative policy advisers in his National Security Strategy in 1999 to going it alone. The conservative turn, the majority in both chambers of Congress in 1994, forced Clinton – according to the AEI's proposals – to increase defense spending, to limit commitment in international organizations, to maintain and enlarge military alliances, with emphasis on the NATO-enlargement in Eastern Europe, to raise military aid and to conduct an aggressive sanctions policy not only towards Iraq but also to other rogue nations like Iran, Libya, Sudan, North Korea and Cuba.

Clinton had thus to refrain from "assertive multilaralism" and give up co-operation with allies and the consideration of their interests. He used since 1997 the option of unilateral military actions for the enforcement of the Iraq sanctions and the tracking of Osama bin Laden in Sudan and in Afghanistan. Henceforth, national security determined his foreign policy.[314] In October 1999 the US Congress decided for the first time in his presidency to raise defense spending.[315]

According to elite theory the Republican Congress promoted the hegemonic and unilateral understanding of US interests that favoured the arms industry and ignored the interest of the American people in peace and disarmament. Before the impeachement Clinton wanted to utilise the budget surplus for saving social security[316], but neoconservative hardliners brought him into line with re-armament and military strength.[317] The president deferred during the divided government to the unilateral definition of national interests by the Republicans since the institutional dissent and strict partisan polarisation did not only put to question his leadership in foreign policy and readjusted the decision-making process to its constitutional limits, but also menaced to paralyse the working of government. His room for manoeuvre was substantially constrained. Instead of collective peace-keeping in a multilateral framework the Republicans in Congress put forward the unilateral US leadership in the world.[318] Therefore, the decision-making already shifted under Clinton from the State Department to the Pentagon as demanded by Republicans.

Clinton signed the Missile Defense Act in 1999 that planned the construction of National Missile Defense (NMD). Disregarding future disarmament negotiations with Russia most notably the prolongation of the ABM-treaty that

[314] Czempiel, Ernst-Otto: „Die stolpernde Weltmacht". Aus Politik und Zeitgeschichte B 46 (2003), pp. 7-15.

[315] Hennis, „ Militärisch-Industrielle Komplex",p. 41.

[316] Blumenthal, Sidney: The Clinton Wars. New York, Farrar, Straus & Giroux 2003,p. 377.

[317] Rosemary Foot, S. Neil MacFarlane and Michael Mastanduno: "Introduction". Rosemary Foot, S. Neil MacFarlane and Michael Mastanduno (eds.): US Hegemony and International Organizations. The United States and Multilateral Institutions. (Oxford: Oxford University Press 2003), pp. 1-22.

[318] Czempiel, "stolpernde Weltmacht", p. 12.

prohibited the missile defense shield, the Clinton administration agreed on the neoconservative assumption that the NMD was vital to counter North-Korean or Iranian long-range missiles as threat to America's security. Furthermore, the Republican-ruled Senate refused to ratify the Comprehensive Testban Treaty in Octobre 1999. Despite his avowals to multilateralism Clinton left a foreign policy legacy that recommitted the US to "global unilateralism". Not just since 9/11 the USA had been confronted with terror as a new threat to her world power status but Clinton had initially declared the war on terror after the attacks in Saudi Arabia in 1996.[319]

---

[319] Clarke, Richard A.: Against All Enemies.Inside America's War on Terror. New York, Free Press 2004, p. 129.

The Bush Administration

The centralisation of the military decisions in one agency that was very closely associated with the president made it easier for the neoconservatives to influence him. On the structural level the decision-making process in the Pentagon was circumscribed to a select few. The neocons were not obliged to approach the rank and file but gained access to a small number of contacts which sufficed to resonate their ideas within the Bush government.[320]

Vice-President Cheney was the key player in the appointment of leading neoconservatives like Abrams, Armitage, Bolton, Wolfowitz and Perle. Peleg characterises Cheney as policy entrepreneur who was highly amenable for neoconservative proposals. Neither Dick Cheney nor Donald Rumsfeld had a neoconservative tenure. Rather both represented traditional Republican hawks who were receptive to neoconservative views. So both of them had signed the founding charter of the Project for a New American Century. Cheney and Rumsfeld shared its unipolarism and thus were aligned with the neoconservative movement.[321] Hard-line conservatives like Cheney and Rumsfeld would never agree with the balance of power or follow Buchanan in an old-fashioned isolationism. Within the Republican Party they belonged according to Dorrien to a circle of aggressive nationalists in foreign policy.[322] President George W. Bush may be close to the Christian Right and Vice-President Dick Cheney be considered a fiscal conservative. These two factions rival with the neoconservatives for ideological predominance in the GOP but both factions concord with them in the unilateral foreign policy for the adherence of national interests, increased defense spending and going it alone.

Though Donald Rumsfeld was no neoconservative he was closely connected to Paul Wolfowitz, Jeane Kirkpatrick and Richard Perle. Indeed he was a go-between the neoconservatives, the corporations and politicians; he partly orchestrated the support of multinationals and arms producers to the neoconservative movement. Big business became the profiteer of neoconservative ideas that legi-

---

[320] Peleg, Ilan: The Legacy of George W. Bush's Foreign Policy. Moving Beyond Neoconservatism. Boulder, Westview Press 2009,p. 136.
[321] Dorrien, Imperial Designs, p. 3.
[322] Ibid.,p. 89.

timised their interests.[323] Rumsfeld nominated neocons such as Wolfowitz and Feith to senior positions in the DoD.[324] The office of the Vice-President, the Pentagon and the Defense Policy Board were neoconservative strongholds.[325] According to Peleg the assertive hawks Cheney and Rumsfeld influenced George W. Bush's decisions on foreign policy. In the case of Bush one can assess that he had the same opinion on neoconservative thinking. In all probability the President made a decision after consulting his Vice-President while both were increasingly affected by neoconservatives who were incorporated in the Defense and State Departments.[326] While Bush's speeches often included religious terms he always stressed his resolve to unilaterally enhance American power. The resolute stance of Bush jr. was the broadening of his Christian faith based on neoconservatism. The neocons gave him assurance that his failing policies were right despite the loss of public opinion. In conveying his policies to the electorate Bush used the neoconservative argumentation that his promotion of liberty and democracy were identical with American interests.[327]

The neoconservative faction in the Bush administration named itself "Vulcans". Vulcans shared the belief in America's military power and their focus on national security. In their neoconservative interpretation of manifest destiny American power and ideals were forces of good which were based on their sanguinity of America's capability in the future. Disputes over competence between Powell's State Department and Rumsfeld-Wolfowitz' Pentagon induced that the White House intervened to reconciliate which exalted Cheney's impact on decision-making. At the same time James Mann points out that even the Clinton administration attributed less importance to the principles of collective security than its predecessors in the Cold War. The Vulcans are compared to the "Wise Men" after the Second World War or the "Best and Brightest" who conducted the Vietnam War. To put the architects of the global order from Bretton Woods and the UN on par with Cheney, Rumsfeld, Wolfowitz or Armitage only proves Powell's role as an outsider who alone believed in the multilateral world order in the Bush administration. As a consequence the comparison with the "Best and Brightest" around Secretary of Defense MacNamara allows to recapitulate the military failures of the neoconservative hawks.[328]

---

[323] Velasco, Neoconservatives, p. 73.
[324] Ibid., p. 207.
[325] Dorrien, Imperial Designs, p. 2.
[326] Peleg, Legacy of George W. Bush' s Foreign Policy, p. 165.
[327]Skidmore, David : "Understanding the Unilateralist Turn in U.S. Foreign Policy". Foreign Policy Analysis 1 No.2 (2005), pp. 207 -228.
[328] Kakutani, Michiko: "How Bush's Advisers Confront the World. Books of The Times: 'Rise of the Vulcans' by James Mann". The New York Times, March 4 2004.

The Bush Doctrine, the Neoconservative Concept for Primacy?

In contrast to Clinton, Bush and his neoconservative entourage reasoned that the United States had to act unilaterally more often, that the deployment of US forces should only take place to protect vital interests, that the USA should address the menace from China and maybe Russia and that the burden of humanitarian interventions should be left to others. What is more, the Bush administration mistrusted everything that its predecessor Clinton had accomplished with multilateral means.[329] In the neoconservative brain trusts foreign policy in general and the United Nations in particular are not considered a top priority but as field of budget cuts which has been high on the agenda of Congress in its relations to the UN. Initially, neocons did not believe in nation-building.[330]

In the enforcement of the Pax Americana neocons were willing to approve tensions in diplomacy and international law: not the entire UN but its perception as fundament of the "new world order" would fall. From their perspective, this was a liberal illusion that the UN Security Council could exclusively legitimise the use of force or guarantee peace through international law in cooperation with other organizations.[331] Moreover, neocons feared that the international institutions might be misused in an absolutely legal and administrative framework to constrain American power by a sovereign world government that strictly followed international law. By implication neocons are regarded as architects of an interventionist unilateralism because of their endorsement of military conflict settlement.

Neoconservative think tanks like the AEI and the PNAC, whose members included Cheney, Rumsfeld, Perle and Wolfowitz, not only demanded a significant rise in defense spending but also the challenging of regimes that were hostile to American values and interests.[332] "Wolfowitz began drafting the doc-

---

[329] Clarke, Against All Enemies. p. 196.
[330] Arin, Kubilay Yado: Die Rolle der Think Tanks in der US Außenpolitik. Von Clinton zu Bush Jr. Wiesbaden, VS Springer 2013.
[331] Halper and Clarke, America Alone, pp. 40-47.
[332] Homolar-Riechmann, "Pax Americana", pp. 34-35.

trine of pre-emptive attack and unilateralism in 1992." [333] As former member of
the Bush sr. administration Wolfowitz formulated in his time at the AEI and later
at the PNAC, which he co-founded, the Bush Doctrine formerly known as
Wolfowitz Doctrine. The Bush Doctrine combined military strategy with the
spreading of democracy. The United States conceived herself as protector of
champions of freedom, peace and human dignity in their home countries against
tyrants and terrorists. Traditionally the USA envisioned herself as role model and
wanted to disseminate globally her liberal views according to Colin Powell.[334]
American values have universal relevance and their global promotion and acceptance are in America's national interest, asserts Condoleeza Rice. The USA
would only experience extensive freedom of action from the angle of political
realism if she were to avoid entangling alliances and international law.[335]

The perceived need for the preemptive use of military force was part of
the neoconservative belief that US security imposed the burden of global hegemony to safeguard the stability of the world and the promotion of universal values such as freedom and liberalism. The Bush Doctrine augured nothing good
for multilateral cooperation. The nation was free to use force at any time with all
means necessary to face the enemy with the potential to threaten its national security. This doctrine aimed at ending any collective control over US use of force.
[336] In the US Security Strategy from 2002 – based on ideas of the PNAC - the
Bush administration avowed to multilateralism with the limitation that in case of
imminent threat - particularly considering the safety of US citizens and the defense of the homeland - Washington would not consult international organisations but reserve the right to military preemption.

In the war on terror the Republican government thus pursued largely a
unilateral policy to enforce its will in the Middle East. On the pretext of protec-
ting national security the USA rejected to sign multilateral agreements for
strengthening the international ban on violence. George W. Bush thus gave up
the US leadership in multilateral issues for the unilateral conduct of the war on
terror.[337] The unilateral war strategy of the AEI and the PNAC was set against
the multilateral US foreign policy that had built the United Nations and NATO.
A more progressive diplomacy would have kept the international law and con-

---

[333] Coffman, Tom : The American Antecedent in Iraq. Majid Tehranian and Kevin P. Clements
(Eds.): America and the World. The Double Bind. New Brunswick, Transaction Publishers 2005, pp.
3-11.
[334] Powell, Colin : "A Strategy of Partnerships". Foreign Affairs, (2004), 83, Nr. 1,pp. 22- 34.
[335] Rice, Condoleeza: "Promoting the National Interest". Foreign Affairs, (2000) 79, Nr. 1,pp. 45- 62.
[336] Franck, Thomas M. : "What Happens Now? The United Nations after Iraq". American Journal of
International Law (AJIL), Vol. 97 (2003), pp. 607-620.
[337] Tehranian, Majid: "Preface". Majid Tehranian and Kevin P. Clements (Eds.): America and the
World. The Double Bind. New Brunswick: Transaction Publishers 2005, pp. VII-IX.

tinued the international cooperation. The USA could have utilised the UN peace-keeping-missions after 9/11. However, by going it alone Bush infuriated both friends and foes.

The terrorist attacks on September 11 2001 enabled the neoconservative clique around Bush, his staff from the AEI and the founders o PNAC, Cheney, Rumsfeld, Perle and Wolfowitz to realize a kind of a "coup" for achieving their proposals in foreign policy.[338] By declaring a war on terror the US got enmeshed in permanent warfare where peace could not be foreseen. As a result Bush jr. regarded himself unlike Clinton, who had led "unpopular wars" in the Balkans, in Somalia or Haiti, as "wartime president".[339] The Bush administration strived to topple Saddam, to increase the defense budget, to shed the constrictive relations to the European allies, to prevent the rise of a rival power and to advance US primacy to secure US interests and the stability of the world. For the neocons the war on terror lifted financial, legal and institutional barriers such as the budge-tary authority of Congress.[340]

For the realisation of the missile defense shield, an idea of the Heritage Foundation since Reagan's presidency, Bush jr. made a bogeyman out of the rogue nations that legitimised rearmament and "ideological messianism". The axis of evil - Iraq, Iran and North Korea - possessed in his argumentation middle-range missiles and weapons of mass destruction that would pose a threat to US and European security. Unlike Clinton he proposed regime change even though his predecessor had pursued „democratic enlargement".[341]

The real test for "nation-building" was in the Middle East where Bush jr. had committed himself to the democratisation of the region especially in his speech to the AEI several weeks prior to the Iraq war.[342] Shortly after, the neocons were accused of having fabricated a "noble myth" about weapons of mass destruction whereby they were also criticised for their Machevellian thinking.[343] According to Buchanan the neocons had captured the conservative movement and Bush's foreign policy for changing with Wilsonian interventions the world in America's image.[344] "Most Neocons would agree that a country's reputation

---

[338] Halper, Stefan/ Clarke, Jonathan : America Alone. The Neo-Conservatives and the Global Order. Cambridge: Cambridge University Press 2004, p. 9.
[339] Ibid., p. 15.
[340] Prestowitz, Clyde: Rogue Nation: American Unilateralism and the Failure of Good Intentions. New York, Basic Books 2003, p. 47.
[341] Pfaff, William: „Die Verselbständigung des Militärischen in der amerikanischen Politik". Blätter für deutsche und internationale Politik, (2001), 2, pp. 177–196.
[342] Micklethwait and Wooldridge, The Right Nation, p. 219.
[343] Ibid., p. 221.
[344] Buchanan, Patrick J.: Where the Right Went Wrong. How Neoconservatives Subverted the Reagan Revolution and Hijacked the Bush Presidency, New York: St. Martin's Press 2004, p. 250.

and perceived status in the world must be taken into account in arriving at realis-
tic policies, but like Machiavelli they contend that a state should want others to
fear it, not necessarily to love or respect it." [345] The Bush administration pro-
ceeded unilaterally against other states for the preservation of the US national
interest in security. While multilateral cooperation under US hegemony was
widely desirable, unilateralism provoked counterveiling power among France,
Germany, Russia, and China or the group of states, the G-77. [346] Their vetoes and
political reactions were directed against the US going it alone and the coalitions
of the willing to execute their „national interests" at cost of other states and the
international law.

The neoconservative attempts for primacy evoked among American allies
the pursuit of their national interests. Particularly Russia and China were reacting
to restrict the unilateralism of the Bush administration. Their use of military
force was shaped in keeping with the US approach in foreign relations; the UN's
monopoly on legitimate use of force was no longer universally valid. "The
alliance of realpolitik with a value-based foreign policy is one of the hallmarks
of neoconservative thought; the end is so noble - the preservation and enhance-
ment of the only power capable of leading the world in a positive direction - that
rea-list means are fully justified." [347]

The neoconservatives saw the occupation of Iraq as first phase in the reordering of the Near East. "By 1997 the neoconservative think-tank the New
American Century Project advocated a remaking of the Middle East."[348] In its
analysis, the Iraq war should secure democracy in the world. Iraq should become
the first democratic state in the Arab world and induce its neighbours to emulate
its progress. Islamism would lose ground since economic prosperity and democratic freedom were contagious. America's military presence would have according to neocons a sobering effect on the authoritarian regimes in the region.
Though the neocons primarily made the same experience like all proponents of
earlier foreign policy doctrines about the frailness of their abstract theories to
real events. The Arab Spring in Tunisia, Egypt and Libya proved the veracity of
their assumptions after years of fighting in Iraq and Afghanistan and months-
long air attacks to oust Gaddafi from power, according to the neoconservative

---

[345] Skillen, With or Against the World, 136.
[346] Jäger, Thomas: „Hypermacht und Unilateralismus. Außenpolitik unter George W. Bush". Blätter
für deutsche und internationale Politik, July 2001, pp. 837–846.
[347] Mead, Walter Russell: Power, Terror, Peace and War. America's Grand Strategy in a World at
Risk. New York: Knopf 2004, p. 90.
[348] Coffman, American Antecedent in Iraq, p. 5.

Hoover Institution.[349] An inexperienced president had to make difficult decisions after 9/11 and thus listened to the advise of his inner circle whom he had recruited from the PNAC. This neoconservative think tank and the Bush administration formed an alliance.[350] Behind the scenes the lobbyists of the arms industry interacted through their scholars with the Congressmen to influence bills in their favor.[351] Furthermore critics recognised in the astronomical foreign debt of the US an increasing menace in the context of the unilateral und military agenda that would effect "imperial overstretch". In their opinion, neoconservatives in the government had used the Iraq war to implement the special interests of the oil industry, of the Israel lobby and the military-industrial complex disregarding the interests of the American people. With the aid of their advisers, Rumsfeld and Cheney, the military-industrial complex had ruled under Bush, opponents claimed.[352]

---

[349] Lagon, Mark P./ Schultz, William F.: "Conservatives, Liberals, and Human Rights". Policy Review, No. 171 Febr. 1 2012. www.hoover.org/publications/policy-review/article/106486 [Accessed Febr. 5 2013]

[350] Abelson, Capitol Idea, p. 10.

[351] Dye, Thomas R.: Top Down Policymaking. New York, Chatham House Publishers 2001, pp. 94 - 102.

[352] Hennis, „neue Militärisch-Industrielle Komplex", p. 46.

The Neoconservative Think Tanks, an Advocacy Coalition?

Following Sabatier's und Jenkins-Smith's explanatory approach the ‚advocacy coalition'[353] neoconservatives have used their network of scholars, journalists, managers, bureaucrats and politicians to convince the foreign policy novice George W. Bush of their plans for the reordering of the Near East. Since the foundation of the PNAC in 1997 the scholars exchanged views with the Republican members of Congress in testimonies. Even before the election of Bush they could convey their unilateral stance not only to Republicans but also to the Clinton administration. Though they did not ultimately succeed under Clinton. Not until Buh jr. came into office the neoconservatives were able under the leadership of their proponents Rumsfeld and Cheney to implement their unilateral pursuit of US primacy, the invasions of Afghanistan and Iraq and the proclamation of the Bush Doctrine. Once in government they isolated dissenters like Colin Powell in the decision-making. As former think-tank scholars they provided Bush jr. with analyses, ideology and knowledge for his plans to topple Saddam Hussein. There existed a coalition of interest and knowledge between the former scholars and their employer in the White House causing a learning effect and the socialisation of neoconservative ideas over group boundaries into the entire state apparatus and to the GOP resulting in a policy change. As a consequence a symbiosis of knowledge and power linked neoconservatives to the Bush administration and the Republican Congress.

One feature of the neoconservative world order was unipolarity, the uncontested primacy of the lone super power. Bill Clinton had initially announced „assertive multilateralism" but conceded priority to US military power whereof George W. Bush relentlessly cherished. The US primacy depended on a military advance that exceeded the combined defense budgets of her 10 most important economic and political adversaries. In this context, Samuel P. Huntington stated: "A world without U.S. primacy will be a world with more violence and disorder

---

[353] Sabatier , Paul A/ Jenkins-Smith, Hank C. (Ed.): Policy Change and Learning. An Advocacy Coalition Approach. Boulder, Westview Press 1993.

and less democracy and economic growth than a world where the United States continues to have more influence than any other country in shaping global affairs."[354] The changes in international politics led to a recalibration of the US role as hegemon in a multipolar to primacy in a unipolar system which resulted in an alignment of the decision-making process in foreign policy. So the USA succumbed to the temptation to maintain and enhance by military means her position as hegemonic power in the world economy. By conducting the war on terror the political elites pursued their goal of universal dominion under Bush jr. After the dismissal of key neoconservatives from the Bush administration the unilateral foreign policy was altered. The alliance between the neoconservative PNAC and the administration ended after the loss of majority in Congress in 2006 whereupon leading neoconservatives like Rumsfeld, Perle and Wolfowitz resigned and their think tank PNAC was closed.[355]

At the end of Bush's term Condoleeza Rice was appointed Secretary of State which marked a policy change. The Bush administration took a moderate position referring to the nuclear proliferation in North Korea, the containment of Iran and the negotiations in the Mideast conflict. Washington made diplomatic instead of military efforts. The US government got involved in the Six-Party talks on the Korean peninsula. Concerning Iran it started a multilateral strategy in the UN-Security Council for preventing Teheran of acquiring a nuclear bomb. In the peace talks in the Near East the USA consulted with Russia, the EU and the UN in the newly-founded Middle East Quartet.[356]

Realists like Colin Powell and Condoleeza Rice shared with the neoconservatives their commitment for US primacy nonetheless they looked for support in the international community for practical reasons. Both argued that cooperation within the world body would spread risks and costs. They had no illusion that multilateralism would provide moral authority; however they advocated that a cooperative UN would arouse less discontent in the community of states. The diplomatic attempts to mediate with Iran, North Korea and the Mideast conflict under Rice created a more positive atmosphere since the Iraq war in 2003.

The new foreign policy should secure the military and economic strength after the loss of the "unipolar moment" (Charles Krauthammer) for shaping a global consensus and mutual agreement with the allies to face global

---

[354] Huntington, Samuel P.: "Why International Primacy Matters". International Security, 1993, 17 (4),pp. 68–83.
[355] Reynolds, Paul: "End of the Neo-con Dream". BBC News Dec. 21. 2006. http://news.bbc.co.uk/go/pr/fr/-/2/hi/middle_east/6189793.stm [Accessed: Jan. 21 2013]
[356] Peleg, Legacy of George W. Bush' s Foreign Policy, p. XII.

challenges under US leadership.[357] Even liberal internationalists contended: multilateralism when possible, going it alone when necessary.[358] In this sense, Nye points to "smart power" that combines strategies of hard and soft power for providing US foreign policy the diplomatic legitimacy of military interventions through the promotion of democracy, human rights and the development of civic society. The war on terror had lessened the "smart power" of the US and after 9/11 brought an "overmilitarised" foreign policy with deep cuts in foreign aid and the budget of the State Department. [359] This is related to the impact of neoconservative think tanks AEI and PNAC which as sectional interest groups defined expansive foreign policy goals at cost of broadly-conceived national interests. As a result the assertive multilateralism of the Clinton administration shifted to unilateral primacy under Bush jr.

The neoconservatives had formed a "counterestablishment" out of think tanks, interest groups and journals that initially should restrict the influence of the liberal establishment.[360] According to Gary Dorrien the neocons still represent the strongest foreign policy faction in the GOP. They are allied with the Christian Right who is lacking an own foreign policy strategy. The neocons are rooted in the Pentagon and the arms industry.[361] Their network in think tanks, government agencies, economy and media such as Fox News will not diminish in the coming years.[362] „In 2009, some of the same people started the Foreign Policy Initiative. Many of Romney's key advisers have been drawn from this network and are credited by him with influencing his outlook".[363] Out of Romney's 24 foreign policy advisers, 17 had worked for the Bush administration. As his advisers the neocons formulated Romney's uncompromising stance towards Russia, China, Iran and the stalled Mideast peace process. Once again, the right-wing intellectuals made the headlines with their impact on American foreign policy.[364]

---

[357] Nye Jr., Joseph S.: The Future of Soft Power in U.S. Foreign Policy. Inderjeet Parmar and Michael Cox (Eds.): Soft Power and U.S. Foreign Policy. Theoretical, Historical and Contemporary Perspectives. London, Routledge 2010, pp. 4-11

[358] In that regard Maull quotes Joseph S. Nye one of the most influential representatives of this school of thought. Maull, . Hanns W: "The Quest for Effective Multilateralism and the Future of Transatlantic Relations". Foreign Policy in Dialogue, Vol 8, Issue 25, pp. 9–18.

[359] Nye Jr., Future of Soft Power, pp. 9-11.

[360] Micklethwait and Wooldridge: The Right Nation, p.382.

[361] Peleg, Legacy of George W. Bush' s Foreign Policy, p. 268.

[362] Ibid., p. 235.

[363] Judis, John B.: "Mitt Romney, Latter-Day Neocon". The New Republic, Sept. 13. 2012.

[364] Berman, Ari: „Mitt Romney's War Cabinet". The Nation May 21 2012. Horowitz, Jason: "Romney's Attacks on Obama Foreign Policy Show Neocons' Dominance". The Washington Post, Sept. 13. 2012. Heilbrunn, Jacob: "Mitt Romney's Neocon Foreign Policy". The National Interest, April 2, 2012.

Conclusion: American Politics and the War of Ideas

In the "war of ideas" think tanks transformed their mission fundamentally from neutral policy advise to administrations, that facilitated decision-making, to lobby organisations that, in reality, solve a multiplicity of domestic and international problems.[365] Thus, advocacy think tanks became actors in policymaking with their own agenda that could be implemented with the aid of their network in all governmental branches, in the economy and in media.[366] Policymakers and their advisers are deeply integrated in a network that in the war of ideas provides their scholars with omnipresence in op-ed articles and interviews in the media and at universities. Different think tanks teach, inform and occasionally lobby among members of Congress, of the executive, of the bureaucracy but also of the media corps.[367]

More problematic seems to be the question of financial and institutional independence of research institutes from corporate and governmental interests in the increasing polarisation of political parties. Though their tax-exempt status as non-profit organisations requests institutional independence, the degree of interference with academic research and the financial support for selective studies raises concerns for the adherence of scientific standards. Nevertheless, the expertise of scholars is needed to translate the technical terminology for the better understanding of the politicians and the electorate. Like universities without students, think tanks educate the public by offering their expert knowledge to practitioners in media, government and economy.[368]

To assert their influence on American politics against the competition of unionists and environmentalists, think tanks devote much of their time and work to media presence not just for drawing the attention of politicians and for distri-

---

[365] Landers, Robert K.: Think-Tanks: The New Partisans? Editorial Research Reports, Congressional Quarterly, 1 (23) 20 June 1986, pp. 455 –472.

[366] Abelson, Donald E.: American Think-Tanks and their Role In US Foreign Policy. London, MacMillan Press Ltd. 1996, p. 64.

[367] McGann James G.: Academics to Ideologues: A Brief History of the Public Policy Research Industry. Political Science and Politics. Vol. 25. No.4 (Dec. 1992), pp. 733- 740 (p. 737). In: www.jstor.org/stable/419684.

[368] Stone, Diane: Capturing the Political Imagination. Think Tanks and the Policy Process. London, Frank Cass 1996, pp. 15-16.

buting their ideas but their degree of popularity raises the amount of donations.[369] So long as their donors are willing to promote their agenda by using the
political connections of think tanks, these research institutes will prosper.[370] That
is why the unlimited access to decision-makers who are open to their proposals
may constitute their most precious resource.[371] In pluralist view, politicians act
as referees in the war of ideas though think tanks outrival the interest groups in
their budgets, their staff, their media presence, and their connections to power
holders.[372]

The research focuses on think tanks, interest groups, foundations,
individual donors, and the role of experts and ideas in the American policy
process.[373] This thesis looked at the elite regroupment of neoconservatives
against liberals with a concern on the polarisation of American politics and its
implications for the American democracy. In my thesis, I analysed the influence
of think tanks, elite policy planning organisations, on US foreign policy.[374] To
facilitate the placement of their staffs advocacy think tanks such Heritage maintain a job bank of key government posts in hope that its former staffers will continue to sell Heritage's neoconservative agenda after taking over power.[375]

More recently, authors such as James Smith, R. Kent Weaver, Howard
Wiarda, Thomas Dye, William Domhoff and Joseph Peschek have focused on
the politicisation of thinks in the 1970s and 1980s. The basic promise is that public policy think tanks, once the fountain of reasoned discourse and dictums on
public policy have become armies of ideologues fighting a war of ideas. The
emergence of advocacy think tanks and their overtly partisan and ideological
reorientation rejecting the consensus for the primacy of their ideas and values.
The politicisation of think tanks became an issue when conservatives entered the

---

[369] Braml, Josef: Deutsche und amerikanische Think Tanks. Voraussetzungen für ihr Wirken.
Wissenschaft und Frieden 2004 – 4: Think Tanks. In www.wissenschaft-und-
frieden.de/seite.php?artikelIld=0337, pp. 1-5 (p. 3).
[370] Abelson, Donald E.: A Capitol Idea. Think Tanks and U.S. Foreign Policy. Montreal 2006, p. 231.
[371] Gehlen, Martin: Kulturen der Politkberatung – USA. In: Bröchler, Stephan/ Schützeichel, Rainer
(eds.): Politikberatung. Stuttgart 2008, pp. 480 – 492 (p. 487).
[372] Jacobs, Lawrence R./ Page, Benjamin I.: Who Influences U.S. Foreign Policy? The American
Political Science Review, Vol. 99, No. 1 (Febr. 2005); pp. 107 – 123 (p. 121). In: www.
jstor.org/stable/30038922 [March 31st 2009]
[373] Abelson, Donald E. A Capitol Idea: Think Tanks and U.S. Foreign Policy. Montreal and
Kingston: McGill-Queen's University Press, 2006.
[374] Abelson, Donald E. "Think Tanks in the United States," in Diane Stone, Andrew Denham and
Mark Garnett (eds), Think Tanks Across Nations: A Comparative Approach. Manchester:
Manchester University Press, 1998: 107-126. Abelson, Donald E. and Evert A. Lindquist. "Think
Tanks Across North America," in R. Kent Weaver and James G. McGann (eds), Think Tanks and
Civil Societies: Catalyst for Ideas and Action. New Jersey: Transaction Publishers, 2000: 37-66.
[375] McGann, James G.: The Competition for Dollars, Scholars and Influence in the Public Policy
Research Industry . Lanham, University Press of America, 1995, p. 132.

market place of ideas. Like Domhoff and Dye, Peschek contends that think tanks are controlled by corporate America, which uses them to control the public policy process and has an undue influence on policymakers in Washington D.C. While former AEI fellow Howard Wiarda disapproves of elite theory and points out that think tanks are responding to the increased competition between political parties that resulted from Republican gains and the emergence of neoconservatism in American politics.[376]

An observer of American think tanks, Nelson Polsby, makes a distinction between the research institutes making a policy impact and think tanks engaging in purely intellectual enterprise. Polsby's approach is rooted in the liberal distinction between the intellectual and the policy sphere whereas conservatives define think tanks namely through their relationship with the state/ policy sphere where the line between policy entrepreneur and politician is blurred. Patronage-client relationships are thus considered never politically illegitimate. The scientific quality of the research produced is not at all diminished by the use of industry or private vested interest made to put pressure on government. In American political thought think tanks are normally considered to be independent from the government. As component of civil society, research institutes fulfil their role as marketers of ideas. Intrusion of the administration in abolishing tax exempt donations is perceived as fundamental affront to the marketplace of ideas, the freedom of science, of thought and speech.[377]

How does the foreign policy establishment, the think tank scholars and academia, interact in emerging issues on national security, human rights, civil liberties and unilateral or multilateral approaches in US Foreign Policy?[378] Think Tanks educate, inform und partially lobby among government representatives, members of Congress, high-ranking bureaucrats and journalists. Politicians and their advisers are deeply integrated in networks.[379] The political reality in the nation's capital contradicted according to James McGann these assumptions. As Brookings was allied with the Democratic Party. The AEI had close ties to the GOP. The once-dominant Brookings had lost its leadership under Reagan, and had to swing to the right to recoup lost ground while the AEI was seen in the mid 1980s too moderate, too centrist. Heritage attacked it on the right as not being conservative enough in order to lure away its more conservative supporters,

[376] Ibid, pp. 20-21.
[377] Polsby, Nelson: Tanks but no Tanks. Public Opinion, April- May 1983, pp. 14-16.
[378] Abelson, Donald E. "What Were They Thinking? Think Tanks, the Bush Administration and U.S. Foreign Policy," in Inderjeet Parmar, Linda B. Miller and Mark Ledwidge (eds), New Directions in US Foreign Policy. London: Routledge, 2009: 92-105.
[379] Abelson, Donald E. "Think Tanks and U.S. Foreign Policy: An Historical View." U.S. Foreign Policy Agenda: An Electronic Journal of the U.S. Department of State, 7 (3), November 2002: 9-12.

while Brookings denounced it from the left in an attempt to capture some of its
more centrist supporters. Heritage did the greatest damage to AEI by effectively
targeting conservative academics, funders and policymakers. Until the mid-
1980s large donors like the Olin-Foundation withdrew their support from AEI.
Competition increased poor management. Lack of endowment changed the political climate. The brain drain was brought on by Reagan's recruiting away AEI
scholars. All factors contributed to its downward spiral.[380]

Over the years, right-wing foundations like Lynde, Bradley, Carthage
and Koch, have not only promoted think tanks but also the university education
of conservative students to journalists, lobbyists, policy experts, economists and
lawyers. As loyalists of free-market economics this right-wing vanguard should
carry their donors' conservative agenda with the Republican Party to Capitol Hill
and into the White House. This rightist intelligentsia worked for the conservative
media tycoon Murdoch, in think tanks and political action committees to accom-
plish a right-ward turn in American politics.[381]

While liberals focus their priorities in the advancement of living condi-
tions for all Americans class through Medicare, social security and equal rights,
Conservatives are obsessed with preserving the economic and political privileges
of the power elites. For electoral success Republicans provoked the fears of
white Americans toward ethnic minorities, communists, homosexuals, immi-
grants and terrorists. National security was the excuse for the constraint of civil
liberties. Economic prosperity justified a sometimes racist undertone. The welfare state was equalised to criminal misconduct, what helped Republicans to get
a mandate.[382]

Rightist think tanks have reshaped the national debate. With their conservative ideas of privatising social security they may not be welcome at leftist
universities but their demand of limited government meets the interests of the
media, the public and their corporate donors despite liberal policymaking.[383]
Because of a greater purse, conservative institutes have won the war of ideas.
Conservative institutes had convinced right-wing foundations to finance their
activities. What turned the balance was according to John C. Goodman, National

---

[380] McGann, James G.: The Competition for Dollars, Scholars and Influence in the Public Policy
Research Industry . Lanham, University Press of America, 1995, pp.123-127.
[381] Covington, Sally: How Conservative Philanthrophies and Think Tanks Transform US Policy.
Covert Action Quarterly 1998. In: www.thirdworldtraveler/Democracy/ConservThinkTanks.html
[October 14th, 2009].
[382] Gonzales, Manuel G./Delgado, Richard: The Politics of Fear. How Republicans Use Money, Race,
and the Media to Win. Boulder, Paradigm Publishers, 2006, p. VIII.
[383] DeMuth, Christopher (Präsident): American Enterprise Institute. In: McGann, James G.: Think
Tanks and Policy Advice in the United States: Academics, Advisors and Advocates. New York,
Routledge 2007 pp. 77- 79 (p. 78).

Center for Policy Analysis, the adoption of corporate marketing and sales strategies. The idea factories converted from research institutes to corporations.[384] Think tanks scholars are not only viewed as objective academics who give neutral advise to government but as policy entrepreneurs who are allied with power blocs, foundations, corporations and political orientations. In addition, these policy experts are advocating an ideological change and a political reorientation. This argumentation can be seen in the writing of liberal critics like Dan T. Carter, Alan Crawford, Thomas Edsall, Michael Lind, Godfrey Hodgson, Paul Krugman, Manuel Gonzales and Richard Delgado.[385] For instance, political parties established strong ties to think tanks, in the case of the Democratic Party to the Brookings Institution and in that of the Republican to the Heritage Foundation and the American Enterprise Institute from Reagan to Bush Jr.[386]

Both in the political transformation under Clinton and the international crises after 9/11 under Bush tragic events were manipulated in their corporate, media and policy clients' interests. In this context, the thesis examined think tanks and their practice of American democracy in areas of foreign relations and national security. Policy proposals from think tanks are related to real-world developments that effected the polarisation of American politics. Consent to policymaking is given by elected officials though they look for policy advise from think tank scholars. Although their influence may be limited to the construction of the agenda, they initiate policy alternatives and facilitate the public understanding of foreign policy issues through their ideas. They act as brain trusts in US foreign policy. In the end, legislators are responsible for the selection and implementation of new policy ideas.[387]

---

[384] Goodman, John C.: What is a Think Tank? National Center for Policy Analysis. Dec. 20th 2005. In: www.ncpa.org/pub/special/20051220-sp.html [October 15th.2009].

[385] Gonzales, Manuel G./Delgado, Richard: The Politics of Fear. How Republicans Use Money, Race, and the Media to Win. Boulder, Paradigm Publishers, 2006, S. VIII.

[386] Stone, Diane/ Garnett, Mark: Introduction: Think Tanks, Policy Advice and Governance. In. Stone, Diane/ Denham, Andrew/ Garnett, Mark (eds.): Think Tanks Across Nations. Manchester, Manchester University Press 1998, S. 1-20, (hier: S. 8).

[387] Stone, Diane: Capturing the Political Imagination. Think Tanks and the Policy Process. London, Frank Cass 1996, p. 2f.

Bibliography

Abelson, Donald E./ Carberry, Christine M.: Policy Experts in Presidential Campaigns. A Model of Think Tank Recruitment. Presidential Studies Quarterly, 1997, 27 (4), pp. 679 – 697.

Abelson, Donald E. A Capitol Idea: Think Tanks and U.S. Foreign Policy. Montreal and Kingston: McGill-Queen's University Press, 2006.

Abelson, Donald E. Think Tanks in the United States, in Diane Stone, Andrew Denham and Mark Garnett (eds), Think Tanks Across Nations: A Comparative Approach. Manchester: Manchester University Press, 1998: 107-126.

Abelson, Donald E. and Evert A. Lindquist. Think Tanks Across North America, in R. Kent Weaver and James G. McGann (eds), Think Tanks and Civil Societies: Catalyst for Ideas and Action. New Jersey: Transaction Publishers, 2000: 37-66.

Abelson, Donald E.: Do Think Tanks Matter? Assessing the Impact of Public Policy Institutes. 2nd Edition. Montreal, McGill-Queen's University Press 2009.

Abelson, Donald E. "In the Line of Fire: Think Tanks, the War on Terror and Anti-Americanism," in Richard Higgott and Ivana Malbasic (eds), The Political Consequences of Anti-Americanism. London: Routledge, 2008, pp. 44-57.

Abelson, Donald E. "A War of Ideas: Think tanks and Terrorism Policy Options, 28 (3) March 2007, pp. 75-78.

Abelson, Donald E. Think Tanks and U.S. Foreign Policy: A Historical View. U.S. Foreign Policy Agenda: An Electronic Journal of the U.S. Department of State, 7 (3), November 2002, pp. 9-12.

Abelson, Donald E. "From Policy Research to Political Advocacy: The Changing Role of Think Tanks in American Politics." The Canadian Review of American Studies 25 (1) Winter 1995: 93-126.

Abelson, Donald E. "What Were They Thinking? Think Tanks, the Bush Administration and U.S. Foreign Policy," in Inderjeet Parmar, Linda B. Miller and Mark Ledwidge (eds), New Directions in US Foreign Policy. London: Routledge, 2009: 92-105.

Abelson, Donald E. "From Policy Research to Political Advocacy: The Changing Role of Think Tanks in American Politics." The Canadian Review of American Studies 25 (1) Winter 1995: 93-126.

Arin, Kubilay Yado: Die Rolle der Think Tanks in der US Außenpolitik. Von Clinton zu Bush Jr. Wiesbaden, VS Springer 2013.

Berman, Ari: „Mitt Romney's War Cabinet". The Nation May 21 2012.

Blumenthal, Sidney: *The Clinton Wars.* New York, Farrar, Straus & Giroux 2003.

Braml, Josef: Deutsche und amerikanische Think Tanks. Voraussetzungen für ihr Wirken. Wissenschaft und Frieden 2004 – 4: Think Tanks. In www.wissenschaft-und-frieden.de/seite.php?artikelIId=0337, pp. 1-5. [July 31st, 2009]

Buchanan, Patrick J.: Where the Right Went Wrong. How Neoconservatives Subverted the Reagan Revolution and Hijacked the Bush Presidency, New York, St. Martin's Press 2004.

Clarke, Richard A.: Against All Enemies.Inside America's War on Terror. (New York: Free Press 2004)

Coffman, Tom: "The American Antecedent in Iraq". Tehranian, Majid and Clements, Kevin P. (eds.): America and the World. The Double Bind. (New Brunswick: Transactions 2005), 3-11.

Covington, Sally: How Conservative Philanthrophies and Think Tanks Transform US Policy. Covert Action Quarterly 1998. In: www.thirdworld traveler/Democracy /ConservThinkTanks. html [Oct. 14 th, 2009].

Crichtlow, Donald T.: The Conservative Ascendancy. How the Republican Right Rose to Power in Modern America. 2. edn. (Lawrence: University Press of Kansas 2011),

Czempiel, Ernst-Otto: „Die stolpernde Weltmacht". Aus Politik und Zeitgeschichte B 46 (2003), pp. 7-15.

DeMuth, Christopher (President): American Enterprise Institute. In: McGann, James G.: Think Tanks and Policy Advice in the United States: Academics, Advisors and Advocates. New York, Routledge 2007 pp. 77- 79.

Dorrien, Gary: Economy, Difference, Empire. Social Ethics for Social Injustice. (New York: Columbia University Press 2010).

Dorrien, Gary: Imperial Designs. Neoconservatism and the New Pax Americana. (New York: Routledge 2004).

Dye, Thomas R.: Top Down Policymaking, (New York: Chatham House Publishers 2001).

Easton, Nina J.: Gang of Five: Leaders at the Center of the Conservative Ascendancy. (New York: Simon & Schuster 2000).

Ehrman, John: The Rise of Neoconservatism. Intellectuals and Foreign Affairs 1945 – 1994. New Haven, Yale University Press 1995.

Foot, Rosemary/ S. Neil MacFarlane/ Michael Mastanduno (eds.): Introduction. US Hegemony and International Organizations. The United States and Multilateral Institutions. Oxford 2003, pp. 1-22.

Franck, Thomas M.: "What Happens Now? The United Nations after Iraq". American Journal of International Law (AJIL), Vol. 97 (2003), 607-620.

Glaab, Manuela/ Metz, Almut: Politikberatung und Öffentlichkeit. In: Falk, Svenja (ed.): Handbuch Poltikberatung. Wiesbaden 2006, pp. 161-172.

Gehlen, Martin: Kulturen der Politkberatung – USA. In: Bröchler, Stephan/ Schützeichel, Rainer (eds.): Politikberatung. Stuttgart 2008, pp. 480 – 492.

Gonzales, Manuel G./Delgado, Richard: The Politics of Fear. How Republicans Use Money, Race, and the Media to Win. Boulder, Paradigm Publishers, 2006.

Goodman, John C.: What is a Think Tank? National Center for Policy Analysis. Dec. 20th, 2005. In: www.ncpa.org/pub/special/20051220-sp.html [October 15th.2009].

Goodman, John C. (President): National Center for Policy Analysis. In: McGann, James G.: Think Tanks and Policy Advice in the United States: Academics, Advisors and Advocates. New York, Routledge 2007, S. 117 – 124

Haas, Richard. N.: Think Tanks and U.S. Foreign Policy. A Policy-Maker′s Perspective. In: The Role of the Think Tanks in U.S Foreign Policy. U.S. Foreign Policy Agenda. An Electronic Journal of the Department of State. Vol. 7, No. 3 (Nov. 2002), p. 5-8. In: www. scribd.com/doc/3210628/the-role-of-the-think-tank-in-us-foreign-policy [August 2nd 2009].

Haller, Gert: Die Bedeutung von Freiheit und Sicherheit in Europa und den USA. APuZ, 5-6/2008, pp. 9-14.

Halper, Stefan and Clarke, Jonathan: America Alone. The Neo-Conservatives and the Global Order. (Cambridge: Cambridge University Press 2004).

Hendrickson, Ryan: The Clinton Wars – The Constitution, Congress, and War Powers, Nashville: Vanderbildt University Press, 2002.

Hennis, Michael: Der neue Militärisch-Industrielle Komplex in den USA. APuZ, B46/2003, pp. 41-46.

Higgott, Richard/Stone, Diane: The Limits of Influence: Foreign Policy Think Tanks in Britain and the USA. Review of International Studies, Vol. 20, No.1 (Jan. 1994), pp. 15 –34 . In. www.jstor.org/stable/20097355 [July 31st, 2009].

Heilbrunn, Jacob: "Mitt Romney's Neocon Foreign Policy". The National Interest, April 2, 2012.

Homolar-Riechmann: Pax Americana und die gewaltsame Demokratisierung. Zu den politischen Vorstellungen der neokonservativen Think Tanks. APuZ, B46/2003, pp. 33-40.

Horowitz, Jason: "Romney's Attacks on Obama Foreign Policy Show Neocons' Dominance". The Washington Post, Sept. 13. 2012.

Huntington, Samuel P.: "Why International Primacy Matters". International Security, 1993, 17 (4), 68–83.

Jacobs, Lawrence R./ Page, Benjamin I.: Who Influences U.S. Foreign Policy? The American Political Science Review, Vol. 99, No. 1 (Febr. 2005); pp. 107 – 123 (p. 121). In: www. jstor.org/stable/30038922 [July 31st, 2009].

Jäger,. Thomas: „Hypermacht und Unilateralismus. Außenpolitik unter George W. Bush". Blätter für deutsche und internationale Politik, July 2001, 837–846.

Jervis, Robert: American Foreign Policy in a New Era. New York 2005.

Judis, John B.: "Mitt Romney, Latter-Day Neocon". The New Republic, Sept. 13. 2012.

Kakutani, Michiko: "How Bush's Advisers Confront the World. Books of The Times: 'Rise of the Vulcans' by James Mann". The New York Times March 4 2004.

Katz, Richard S.: Politische Parteien in den Vereinigten Staaten. Fokus Amerika der Friedrich-Ebert-Stiftung Nr.7, Washington, DC 2007.

Kingdon, John W.: Agendas, Alternatives and Public Policies. Boston, Little, Brown & Company, 1984.

Krugman, Paul: Nach Bush. Das Ende der Neokonservativen und die Stunde der Demokraten. (Bonn: Bundeszentrale für politische Bildung 2008).

Kuttner, Robert: "Philanthrophy and Movements". The American Prospect July 15 2002. www. propect.org/cs/articles?article=philanthropy _and_movements [Accessed Jan. 25 2013].

Laipson, Ellen (Präsident und CEO): The Henry L. Stimson Center. In: McGann, James G.: Think Tanks and Policy Advice in the United States: Academics, Advisors and Advocates. New York, Routledge 2007, pp. 94 – 97.

Lagon, Mark P. and Schultz,William F.: "Conservatives, Liberals, and Human Rights". Policy Review, No. 171 Febr. 1 2012. www.hoover.org/ publications/policy-review/article/106486 [Accessed Febr. 5 2013]

Landers, Robert K.: Think-Tanks: The New Partisans? Editorial Research Reports, Congressional Quarterly, 1 (23) 20 June 1986, pp. 455 –472.

Luck, Edward C.: "American Exceptionalism and International Organisation: Lessons from the 1990s". Rosemary Foot/ S. Neil MacFarlane and Michael Mastanduno (eds.): US Hegemony and International Organizations. The United States and Multilateral Institutions. (Oxford: Oxford University Press 2003), 25-48.

Maull, Hanns W.: "The Quest for Effective Multilateralism and the Future of Transatlantic Relations". Foreign Policy in Dialogue, Vol 8, Issue 25, 9–18.

McGann James G.: Academics to Ideologues: A Brief History of the Public Policy Research Industry. Political Science and Politics. Vol. 25. No.4 (Dec. 1992), pp. 733- 740 (p. 737). In: www.jstor.org/stable/419684 [March 31st, 2009].

McGann, James G.: The Competition for Dollars, Scholars and Influence in the Public Policy Research Industry. Lanham, University Press of America, 1995.

McGann, James G.: Think Tanks and Policy Advice in the United States: Academics, Advisors and Advocates. New York, Routledge 2007.

Mead, Walter Russell: Power, Terror, Peace and War. America's Grand Strategy in a World at Risk. (New York: Knopf 2004),

Micklethwait, John and Wooldridge, Adrian: The Right Nation. Conservative Power in America. (New York: Penguin Books 2004),

Müller, Harald: „Das transatlantische Risiko – Deutungen des amerikanisch-europäischen Weltordnungskonflikts". Aus Politik und Zeitgeschichte B 3-4/ (2004), 43-44.

Nye, Joseph S.: The Future of Soft Power in U.S. Foreign Policy. Inderjeet Parmar and Michael Cox (Eds.): Soft Power and U.S. Foreign Policy. Theoretical, Historical and Contemporary Perspectives. (London: Routledge 2010), 4-11

Nye, Joseph S.: Soft Power. The Means to Success in World Politics. (New York: Public Affairs, 2004).

Newsom, David D.: The Public Dimension of Foreign Policy. Bloomington, Indiana University Press 1996.

Peleg, Ilan: The Legacy of George W. Bush's Foreign Policy. Moving Beyond Neoconservatism. (Boulder: Westview Press 2009).

Peschek, Joseph G.: Policy-Planning Organisations. Elite Agendas and America's Rightward Turn. Philadelphia, Temple University Press 1987.

Pfaff, William: „Die Verselbständigung des Militärischen in der amerikanischen Politik". Blätter für deutsche und internationale Politik, (2001), 2, 177–196.

Prestowitz, Clyde: "Rogue Nation: American Unilateralism and the Failure of Good Intentions". (New York: Basic Books 2003),

Powell, Colin: A Strategy of Partnerships. In: Foreign Affairs, 2004, Jg. 83, Nr. 1, pp 22- 34.

Polsby, Nelson: Tanks but no Tanks. Public Opinion, April- May 1983, pp. 14-16.

Reinicke, Wolfgang H.: Lotsendienste für die Politik: Think Tanks – amerikanische Erfahrungen und Perspektiven für Deutschland. Gütersloh 1996.

Reynolds, Paul: "End of the Neo-con Dream". BBC News Dec. 21. 2006. http://news.bbc.co.uk/go/pr/fr/-/2/hi/middle_east/6189793.stm [Accessed: Jan. 21 2013]

Ricci, David: The Transformation of American Politics. The New Washington and the Rise of Think Tanks. New Haven, Yale University Press, 1993.

Rice, Condoleeza: Promoting the National Interest. In: Foreign Affairs, 2000, Jg. 79, Nr. 1, pp. 45-62.

Rich, Andrew: Think Tanks, Public Policy and the Politics of Expertise. Cambridge, Cambridge University Press 2004.

Rivlin, Benjamin: UN Reform from the Standpoint of the United States: A Presentation Made At The United Nations University on 25 September 1995, Tokyo Japan, UN University Lectures 11. In: www.unu.edu/unupress/lecture11.html

Rhodes, R.A..W./Marsh, David: New Studies in the Study of Policy Networks. European Journal of Policy Research 1992, 21, pp. 181 – 205.

Rubenstein, Richard E.: Die US-amerikanischen Wahlen. Aussichten für eine neue amerikanische Außenpolitik. Fokus Amerika der Friedrich-Ebert-Stiftung (Nr. 2), Washington, DC 2008. p.5-6.

Rudolf, Peter: USA - Sicherheitspolitische Konzeptionen und Kontroversen. In: Ferdowsi, Mir A. (ed.): Sicherheit und Frieden zu Beginn des 21. Jahrhunderts. München 2002, pp. 149- S.163.

Rochefort, David A. and Cobb, Roger W.: The Politics of Problem Definition. Shaping the Policy Agenda. (Lawrence: University Press of Kansas 1994).

Sabatier, P.A./Jenkins-Smith, H.C. (eds.): Policy Change and Learning. An Advocacy Coalition Approach. Boulder, Westview Press, 1993.

Sheffer, Martin S.: Presidential War Powers and the War on Terrorism: Are We Destined to Repeat Our Mistakes? In: Davis, John (ed.): The Global War on Terrorism: Assessing the American Response. New York 2004, pp. 27-44.

Skillen, James W.: With or Against the World? America's Role Among the Nations. Lanham 2005.

Skidmore, David: "Understanding the Unilateralist Turn in U.S. Foreign Policy". Foreign Policy Analysis 1 No.2 (2005), 207 -228.

Smith, James A.: The Idea Broker: Think Tanks and the Rise of the New Policy Elite. New York, Free Press 1991.

Sterling-Folker, Jennifer: "Between a Rock and a Hard Place. Assertive Multilateralism and Post-Cold-War U.S. Foreign Policy". James M. Scott, (Ed.): After the End. Making U.S. Foreign Policy in the Post-Cold-War World. (Durham: Duke University Press 1998), 277 – 304.

Stone. Diane: Introduction. Think Tanks, Policy Advice, and Governance. In: Stone, Diane/ Denham, Andrew (eds.): Think Tank Traditions, Policy Research, and the Politics of Ideas. Manchester, Manchester University Press 2004, pp. 1-16.

Stone, Diane: Capturing the Political Imagination. Think Tanks and the Policy Process. London, Frank Cass 1996.

Stone, Diane/ Denham, Andrew (eds.): Think Tank Traditions, Policy Research, and the Politics of Ideas. Manchester, Manchester University Press 2004.

Tehranian, Majid: "Preface". Majid Tehranian and Kevin P. Clements (Eds.): America and the World. The Double Bind. (New Brunswick: Transaction Publishers 2005), VII-IX.

Thunert, Martin: Think Tanks in Deutschland – Berater der Politik? ApuZ B51/2003, pp. 30 – 38

Tsebelis, George: Veto Players. How Political Institutions Work. Princeton, Princeton University Press 2002.

Velasco, Jesús: Neoconservatives in U.S. Foreign Policy under Ronald Reagan and George W. Bush. Voices Behind the Throne. (Washington D.C.: Woodrow Wilson Center Press 2010).

Wallace, William: Conclusion. Ideas and Influence. In: Stone, Diane/ Denham, Andrew/ Garnett, Mark (Eds.): Think Tanks Across Nations. Manchester, Manchester University Press 1998, pp. 223- 230.

Weller, Christoph: Machiavellistische Außenpolitik - Altes Denken und seine US-amerikanische Umsetzung, In: Hasenclever, Andreas / Wolf, Klaus Dieter / Zürn, Michael (eds.): Macht und Ohnmacht internationaler Institutionen. Frankfurt a.M./New York: Campus, 2007, pp. 81-114.

Weaver, R. Kent: The Changing World of Think Tanks. PS: Political Science and Politics. September 1989, pp. 563 – 578.

Weiss, Carol: Introduction: Helping Government Think: Functions and Consequences of Policy Analysis Organisations. In: Weiss, Carol (Ed.) Organisations for Policy Advice. Helping Government Think. London, Sage 1992, pp. 6-8.

Wiarda, Howard: Conservative Brain Trust. The Rise, Fall, and Rise Again of the American Enterprise Institute. Lanham, Lexington Books, 2009.

Wilson, Hall T.: Capitalism After Postmodernism. Neo-conservatism, Legitimacy and the Theory of Public Capital. Leiden 2002.

VS Forschung | VS Research
Neu im Programm Politik

Michaela Allgeier (Hrsg.)
Solidarität, Flexibilität, Selbsthilfe
Zur Modernität der Genossenschaftsidee
2011. 138 S. Br. EUR 39,95
ISBN 978-3-531-17598-0

Susanne von Hehl
Bildung, Betreuung und Erziehung als neue Aufgabe der Politik
Steuerungsaktivitäten in drei Bundesländern
2011. 406 S. (Familie und Familienwissenschaft) Br. EUR 49,95
ISBN 978-3-531-17850-9

Isabel Kneisler
Das italienische Parteiensystem im Wandel
2011. 289 S. Br. EUR 39,95
ISBN 978-3-531-17991-9

Frank Meerkamp
Die Quorenfrage im Volksgesetzgebungsverfahren
Bedeutung und Entwicklung
2011. 596 S. (Bürgergesellschaft und Demokratie Bd. 36) Br. EUR 39,95
ISBN 978-3-531-18064-9

Martin Schröder
Die Macht moralischer Argumente
Produktionsverlagerungen zwischen wirtschaftlichen Interessen und gesellschaftlicher Verantwortung
2011. 237 S. (Bürgergesellschaft und Demokratie Bd. 35) Br. EUR 39,95
ISBN 978-3-531-18058-8

Lilian Schwalb
Kreative Governance?
Public Private Partnerships in der lokalpolitischen Steuerung
2011. 301 S. (Bürgergesellschaft und Demokratie Bd. 37) Br. EUR 39,95
ISBN 978-3-531-18151-6

Kurt Beck / Jan Ziekow (Hrsg.)
Mehr Bürgerbeteiligung wagen
Wege zur Vitalisierung der Demokratie
2011. 214 S. Br. EUR 29,95
ISBN 978-3-531-17861-5

Einfach bestellen:
SpringerDE-service@springer.com
tel +49 (0)6221 / 3 45 – 4301
springer-vs.de

Printed in Great Britain
by Amazon